Creative IQ

May you find and
Share your creative
gift with the world!

Renee

Creative IQ

Opening the Door to Creativity
that Inspires Sustainable Results

Renee Russo Martinez

NEW DEGREE PRESS

CREATIVE IQ
Opening the Door to Creativity that Inspires Sustainable Results

ISBN
979-8-88926-698-3   *Paperback*
979-8-88926-699-0   *eBook*

To Francisco, Lucas, Mateo, and Gabriel, who are the magic sauce of inspiration in my life. They remind me to live fully, laugh often, and be curious. May love and creativity always fill their lives.

CONTENTS

"Creativity is not just for artists. It's for businesspeople looking for a new way to close a sale; it's for engineers trying to solve a problem; it's for parents who want their children to see the world in more than one way."

—TWYLA THARP

Welcome.

Grab a chair and make yourself comfortable. I'm glad you're here.

The following pages will help you reconnect with your inner child and boost your Creative IQ. Relax. As you plunge in, you'll rediscover the spark that lives within each and every one of us. Release the fear that what you create isn't good enough. Nothing is perfect. Instead, be curious and live like a traveler. You'll find inspiration in the unexpected, and extraordinary in the ordinary. Take the time to enjoy the journey to becoming the most creative version of yourself.
Enjoy!

INTRODUCTION

When I was young, I could get lost in the sky—the cloud formations, the beautiful palette of colors decorating the sky, and the wonder of the unknown. I've always assumed it was some sort of hopeful longing to catch a glimpse of my grandmother, who died far too young. She represented freedom, love, and playfulness to my child's mind. We did simple things like sliding down the stairs on our bums and laughing ourselves silly. In that sense, the unpredictable cloud formations represent a free-spiritedness and a place to lend the mind to wander and the imagination to run wild.

Adults lose the sense of playfulness and creativity, and this impacts happiness, productivity, and clarity. This book will help you reconnect with your inner child and learn how to use it as your superpower both in your personal and professional life.

Creativity has become a buzzword. Yet it feels hollow, like a word repeated too often. In my opinion, creativity is not a process where you can learn the steps. It's about tapping into an inner knowing, being still enough in your mind and aware enough of your environment to hear the tiny inspired moments that reveal themselves to your creative soul. It's only when you have calibrated yourself to be open to creativity that you can begin the process of learning how to use it.

In today's world, we are plugged into a digital reality that can both inspire and minimize our creative voice. As an early adopter of social media, I confess that, while professionally it opened many doors for me—from finding and exploring exciting content to connecting with people and opportunities from all over the globe—the twenty-four-hour access via cell phone also dimmed my awareness outside of the glowing screen. Having my eyes stuck to my phone or laptop prevented me from seeing the world around me as clearly as I did before. I had to adopt a regular practice of mindfulness and meditation to stay tuned in to what's around me.

While professionally, the benefits of this newfound digital world had tremendous value, personally, it had the potential to interfere with running a household and being a mom to four young sons, a wife, a daughter, and a friend. Being disciplined, present, and focused on my time was a skill I had to learn.

My inspiration boards on Pinterest, and all the curated content directed at me, did help me create art, but it also sucked me deeper into the digital abyss. My time spent online felt lonely and isolated. I recalled that, in the pre-handheld device world, I would walk around and observe details, interact live with humans, or be more in touch with nature, which in turn might inspire a thought or an idea. Now, as I walk down the street, I'll check my phone, read as I walk and, often, rarely look up from the screen. It is now possible to completely avoid human contact and lean into virtual existence.

Juggling the roles of parent versus professional has become more challenging as there seems to be no off button for work like there had before. Now my boys are older and, while I'm confident they always knew they were a priority, I never wanted them to compete for my attention with the screen. Looking around today, I see so many parents using the screen as a babysitter for their child. Even more concerning is when I see a child at a restaurant trying to interact with a parent deep into their life on their phone. The need for digital balance is critical today more than ever before.

This digital isolation has compounded post-COVID-19 as more and more people are working remotely. The impact this is having on people's mental health is profound and detrimental. We are social beings for whom a critical component is the ability to create, yet if we are numbed to hearing the inner voice sparking inspiration, we shift our mind from creator to processor; from truly engaging to passively observing.

When I was a young girl, I remember associating positive feedback with the art I would create. I was a talkative and outgoing child filled with energy. When grades began to matter and success meant having an ability to retain and produce the information requested on a test, I began to struggle. My big ideas, which were once valued, began to feel like the very things that were getting in the way. I didn't realize it at the time, of course, but perhaps I was feeling that my creative endeavors were less legitimized than achieving high grades would be. Fluttering between paying attention in school and my crazy ideas, it never felt like I fit in. I wanted to be the ideal student who did my work and got good grades, but school felt confining and boring to me. Eventually, I resorted to accepting I just wasn't a good student.

I've always been a daydreamer, which tends to have a negative connotation. "I wish she'd pay attention and stop daydreaming" was a phrase often uttered to my parents and well-intended teachers. Here's the thing: daydreaming is important. It provides a way for the brain to process self-related information to update our life story. Imagining the stories in our daydreams helps us to make sense of who we are and provides us with the tools to build what's called our narrative identity.

According to Dan McAdams, a professor of psychology at Northwestern University, "It's a story you've got about how you came to be, who you are, and where your life's going. That's not your whole identity—there are a lot of other things that are part of your identity—but it's an important part, and it's a neglected part. Narrative identity is just as much about how you imagine the future, even though it hasn't happened yet, as it is about how you reconstruct the past. If I'm planning to be president of the United States, and I'm currently laboring in academia, well you're going to have to develop a way to connect up your past with your goals for the future" (Sedacca 2019).

I feel there's a deeply spiritual component to this process of creativity. Maintaining awareness of our thoughts, feelings, and sensations in the present moment, without judgment and instead with a kind, calm curiosity, is what mindfulness means to me. It's an acceptance of the here and now and a surrender to "be." Rooted in Buddhist meditation, mindfulness became mainstream through the work of Jon Kabat-Zinn and his Mindfulness-Based Stress Reduction (MBSR) program at the University of Massachusetts Medical School in 1979 (National Gallery of Ireland 2022). Mindfulness is what causes you to have an imaginative spark that enables you to be creative. It is taking time to pause and pay attention to what's happening now. Mindfulness is a judgment-free space that allows us to more deeply connect to where we are and what's going on around us. There are many ways to practice mindfulness, but at the National Gallery of Ireland, they offer mindfulness tours (both in person and online) to help patrons calm their minds by spending time looking at art.

One day, my friend Christina and I decided to visit New Mexico for a last-minute long weekend adventure to escape our young adult lives in Chicago. This was in the early '90s when there were no cell phones or Travelocity. Other than our flights and a car rental, I don't recall booking any accommodations or having any type of plan whatsoever. We were truly winging it and exploring. At some point along the road, beneath the deep blue sky, I felt the long-forgotten inner pull calling me to create. It was both energizing and inspiring.

Maybe I was just channeling Georgia O'Keefe or Agnes Martin, both of whom were led to that magical place and found peace and inspiration there. Maybe it was the deeply rooted Native American culture, rich with artistic inspiration that connected with me on some spiritual level. All I can tell you is that something magical happened. I was in a space where wonder and awe peppered every moment, and I felt this deep sense and desire for more. Without question, with our freedom came creativity.

This awakening turned out to be the beginning of a reconnection with my inner creative self. While I would go on to do a few little shows in local coffee shops here and there, it would be many years later before I was willing to call myself an artist.

When I reflect on the ebb and flow moments of inspiration, it's abundantly clear that true creativity and innovation comes from looking at things differently. That's why, when I removed myself from one environment, such as my trip to New Mexico, everything was new. My mind was propelled to a place of heightened awareness and deep awakening. Essentially, my thinking mind took a break to allow the subconscious an opportunity to bubble up and offer its contributions. So how do you level-up your subconscious contributions without leaving your desk? The next time you say you're in a rut, you're probably right, but your decision to stay and stagnate depends on your willingness to tap into what's around you.

The dilemma is how to access creative potential.

How do we allow ourselves the time to relax, recharge, and find inspiration?

When we function from a place of fear, there's more rigidity in being set in our views. Therefore, it seems our capacity to be open is likely connected to looking beyond our fears. When I interviewed Lindsay Amico, a mindset coach and founder of Picture Perfect Mind, she stated, "It's about identifying the limiting beliefs. You're able to drop back into love and yourself. Owning that work can remove the perceived blocks, and then step you fully into your creativity."

Sometimes it's difficult to allow yourself time to relax, recharge, or find inspiration. It's easy to find excuses—work, kids, adulting, to name a few. Some people wear the word "busy" like a badge of accomplishment to be proud of when it could also be an indication of a person who's unorganized, unfulfilled, unbalanced, or inefficient. Making time for yourself to decompress and destress is critical, not only for your health and wellness but for feeding your creative mind and creating an environment open for inspiration.

Oftentimes, we are paralyzed by our limiting beliefs to the point that we allow our fear of not being good enough or of letting people down—which leads to being a people pleaser—control us and limit our creativity. Once we accept, love, and ultimately own who we are, we can move forward, fully embracing our path and the person we have become. This relinquishes us of our emotional burden and allows us to blossom—honestly and authentically.

We live in a paradoxical world punctuated by the dual nature of human existence and the natural world. There's no day without night, no life without death. The concept of yin and yang stems from a Chinese philosophy called Taoism (Exploring Your Mind 2020). The Tao Te Ching is an ancient piece of writing that is believed to be written by Lao Tau around sixth century. He refers to a "paradoxical unity." We've all experienced highs and lows. There's always an upside or an alternative thought, and this is the paradoxical reality we live in. Good versus evil. Pain or pleasure. There are two sides to every coin. Every failure exists as the counter of success. What the Tao suggests is that we find oneness and unity within these paradoxes, in between the ugly and the beautiful or the happy and the sad. This is a perspective that is not easy to adopt, much less incorporate into your daily perspective, but doing so allows you to accept both sides and that life is created from a balanced interaction of opposite and competing forces.

Therefore, mindfulness plays a critical role in sparking imagination to inspire creativity. However, if all it took was a jolt of mindfulness, then certainly creativity wouldn't be as elusive as it seems to be, nor would it be the hot buzzword for corporations as they seek to infuse creativity and innovation into their organizations.

Theodore Levitt, a German American economist and a professor at the Harvard Business School, is quoted as saying, "What is often lacking is not creativity in the idea-creating sense but innovation in the action-producing sense, i.e., putting ideas to work" (Business Insider 2013). My belief is there's a missing link in the discussion, a prelude to the kiss of creativity that, unless recognized as part of the process, makes creativity simply a word packed with hope.

The purpose of this book is to demonstrate effective ways to dive deeply into creativity as a process, mindfulness to be inspired into the process, and the actions needed to move to innovation starting with the individual.

This book was born out of a place of love and compassion. Whether you think of yourself as an artist or a performer, a creative problem solver or someone who just thinks differently, this book is for you. As the mysteries of creativity unfold, you might find there's an unspoken spiritual aspect to accessing creativity and the actions to go from inspiration to innovation. I feel what you feel, and we are united in our unconventional perspectives and bold ideas.

As a fellow misfit in my own mind, my hope is that this book is the spark you need to propel you into liberating yourself from the chains of your discomfort and gives you the tools to embrace your inner creative genius. To own it, flaunt it, and rock it like you would with that inner voice of "I told you so" after you won a dispute with a friend on an issue you knew you were right about all along.

KEY
TAKEAWAYS
Introduction

- Creativity is like a plant, you need to feed and water it, in order for to produce.

- Making the time to allow yourself to relax and recharge is necessary for maintaining a healthy balance in your life.

- Mindfulness plays a critical role in sparking imagination to inspire creativity.

This is a little painting I created. The unpredictable cloud formations represent a freespiritedness and a place to lend the mind to wander and the imagination to run wild.

This is my Dad and I. His entrepreneurial spirit was a huge inspiration throughout my life.

This is my Grandma. She represented freedom, love, and playfulness to my child's mind.

This little jeep represents the adventure to New Mexico that ignited my creativity.

These are my boys. They remind me to live fully, laugh often, and be curious.

Take a step outside and look up at the sky like you did when you were a child. What stands out to you? The color of the sky? The cloud formations? Using your cell phone, snap a photo and then take a moment to write and reflect on what you saw.

_____

_____

_____

_____

_____

_____

_____

_____

_____

_____

_____

_____

_____

_____

_____

_____

_____

_____

_____

_____

_____

_____

_____

_____

_____

_____

_____

_____

_____

_____

RECONNECTING WITH CREATIVITY

In elementary and high school, I was always the one who was labeled as "doesn't work to fullest potential." If daydreaming was a class, I would have earned an A. I had outlandish, crazy ideas and a little bit of a wild spirit, so my natural instinct was to do something erratic or irrational. That didn't always go over well in my small traditional Catholic school or even among family members, who were always concerned with what other people would think.

I had dark unruly hair in a sea of straight coiffures. I wanted, so desperately, to blend in that I did anything I could to straighten my hair. This was in the days before hair gel, so I either suffered for hours with my mom at the hands of the blow-dryer or looked like I'd been electrocuted.

This culture of criticism that permeated my world taught me to question my own decisions in the context of how others might perceive them. It ushered in a fear of failure and potential disappointment regarding my obtuse ideas in favor of what is safe and free of judgment. I learned to conform, even if it conflicted with who I was, solely for the purpose of feeling accepted.

Growing up, my mother nurtured my imagination and creative curiosity by playing with dolls and drawing with me. From dance to figure skating, art to music, I had a childhood rich in play and artistic expression. My thirst for adventure also started young. I recall taking Sunday drives, going camping, or even just exploring my yard for critters.

I began college as a graphic design major. Then one day, I had a conversation with my father, who questioned my choice, wondering what kind of income I could possibly generate with an art degree, so I changed my major to communication, thinking it was more appropriate for a future in business. I justified my decision by convincing myself I didn't want to lose interest in my love for art as a hobby, when, in reality, I let being a people pleaser extend to even the most critical decision of what I would do in my future.

After graduation, I moved to bustling Chicago and entered the workforce in a marketing capacity. I had limited time for creativity, given the new professional demands of my work and a lukewarm commitment to painting. Not sure how to incorporate a regular art practice, or why doing so would be of any value, I eventually let go of art as my hobby. Apart from a couple pieces hanging at a nearby coffeehouse, my art days were essentially over.

Once my life shifted to the parenthood phase, making time for creative endeavors wasn't even on my radar. I was focused on being a mom and doing marketing consulting. Art in my life during these early parenting years was either in a professional design capacity or with my boys in our art smocks, slinging paints onto paper fastened to an easel I set up to make art a focus in our lives. Ironically, to this point, I had yet to fully appreciate that my quirky curiosity and outlandish ideas were actually strengths.

Speaking of curiosity, my desire for exploration and inquiry led me to the internet as an early adopter of social media. With four young boys and a love for writing, I found myself with a desire to document my journey as a mother in the form of a blog. *Raising Boys World*, a blog about raising boys that began in 2006, led to many exciting opportunities. I stumbled upon the hashtag #UsGuys on Twitter early on in the Twittersphere, where more people started to connect via the hashtag. My world suddenly evolved as I built friendships with people from all over the world. From creating and teaching college-level social media courses to starting a social media conference, I was riding a wave ahead of the curve. Looking back, I can see my lack of confidence hindered my ability to take steps to propel my advantage into a next-level business.

When my husband's job presented a move with our family to a new city, I found myself with an opportunity to pursue a PhD at a highly competitive university that would begin shortly after our move. I had not been a student for many years, and my life was vastly different, as a student and as a person. I had to manage four children, a husband, relocation to a new house, and no network. And it was far more difficult to manage than my superhero-self imagined.

As I started my program, I began to see a shift in what was previously a confident and courageous person to one of facing the demons of my own inadequacies and insecurities associated with my role as a student.

I was accepted into this incredible program. Exactly what I would have wanted. And the little girl inside of me, I realized, was sabotaging my opportunity because, internally, I didn't feel I deserved it. This is imposter syndrome. I've been doing this all my life—never allowing myself a win, never feeling that I deserved it when I received it. My old fears from the past began to creep in, and like algae on a body of water, my vision became clouded, and I felt inadequate.

Imposter syndrome is defined as "the internal psychological experience of feeling like a phony in some area of your life, despite any success that you have achieved in that area" (Cuncic 2022). According to Healthline, "Imposter syndrome, also called perceived fraudulence, involves feelings of self-doubt and personal incompetence that persist despite your education, experience, and accomplishments" (Saripalli 2021). What's more is research suggests approximately 25 to 30 percent of high achievers may suffer from imposter syndrome, with 70 percent of adults likely to experience imposter syndrome at least once in their life (Sakulku and Alexander 2011).

In addition to my new coursework, only six months into my program, my husband lost his job. Suddenly, in addition to being a mom and a student, I assumed the role of personal support and job search to my husband as he navigated looking for a new role. Meanwhile, my father required quadruple bypass surgery, my kids were in competitive sports, and, as if that's not enough, I had a dog that was having aggression and behavioral issues. I could not take on one more thing. My mind couldn't focus. I was diagnosed with ADHD, which answered a lot of questions about my childhood. I went through a process of grieving, to some extent, wondering how my life might have been so different if I'd known earlier or had the tools to deal with the diagnosis.

It was an awful time. Obviously, that would take a huge toll on anyone, but I let that experience destroy my spirit, my drive, and my dreams. I remember feeling that I didn't belong and feeling overwhelmed by trying to juggle everything all at once, so I began to let things slide while I found myself becoming a sadder, more anxious person who felt like giving up.

There are times when it feels like no matter how hard you try to make something work, even when you know it's an incredible opportunity, you just can't make it happen. You just have to let go.

I didn't even recognize the subtle nudge toward claiming my creative self. I wasn't aware of the emotional benefits I received from indulging in regular artistic practice until my world felt like I was running through a cornfield, dodging the thick hearty leaves, overwhelming me with nowhere to go, and whipping me into a fury of anxiety and distress. Sometimes it takes a breakdown of your world to realize you're barely hanging on and you need fresh eyes and a new start.

This idea of failure is so hard. It cuts into you. I have felt that total and complete breakdown, but like most people (especially women), I also didn't feel compelled to ask for help. Instead, I kept moving on, trudging onward. I kept going as if I had everything under control, doing what I thought I was supposed to be doing. While my insides were in knots, my mind was racing, and my emotions were out of control.

I gave up on that opportunity to pursue a PhD. At that point, I was hitting rock bottom. I needed to find something to give me peace. I did not talk to anyone. I didn't talk to any friends about the depths of how I was feeling. I felt that, when I tried to, people would just always say, "Well, you'll be fine. You got it, Renee." It felt like nobody really was listening to me.

My way of managing this shitstorm was initially to kick into high-gear and try to solve every problem I was presented with. Then I felt compelled to go within. At first, I reconnected with the familiar habit of pouring my emotions onto a canvas and painting. It'd been years since I had last dipped the brittles into paint and pulled the wet substance across a canvas. It felt good to my soul. Allowing me to find peace and focus, it was like being reacquainted with a lost familiar friend.

I began to really find peace in the sky. To me, the sky is the great equalizer. It's what connects us as humans. No matter where you live or what you do, we all respond similarly to a beautiful sky as much as we do to an ominous story.

It was as though an inner consciousness was pulling me toward releasing a lot of pent-up creative energy. I reconnected with myself through art, being a mom, and meditation and yoga. I even completed my yoga teacher training during this time so I could share something that had a powerful impact on my mental fitness with others. The break in creating and showing art came to an end as I reclaimed my creativity and shared it again with patrons interested in buying my work. It was an honor to learn my work was connecting with people. And when I again heard that inner voice that questioned if I belonged, I was able to quieten it and instead own up to what I'd done, where I'd been, and where I was going.

KEY
TAKEAWAYS
Chapter 1

- Stress, anxiety, and fear interfere with accessing your inner antenna, but adopting an attitude of acceptance and open-mindedness will position you to receive insights and inspirations. These often feel like an inner nudge or desire to explore something further.

- You charge the antenna by quieting your feelings of self doubt, allowing yourself to feel vulnerable, and asking for help when you need it.

- Start to look at failure as opportunity.

- When you catch yourself making excuses or placing blame on other people, you give away your power.

- Listening to your gut or intuition is a key factor in honing your Creative IQ.

- Allow yourself time to reflect.

- Stop trying to solve everyone's problems and start giving yourself the respect you deserve.

What can you do?

- Start by scheduling 5 minutes in the morning and every evening to just sit in a quiet and peaceful space.

- You can choose what makes you feel calm. It might be prayer, a mantra or just focusing on an object

- You deserve it! Plus, it's a great way to start and finish your day.

If you're like me, you're probably running from one thing to the next without a moment to pause and catch your breath. When you're not committed to doing something, then, like me, you might find you're checking email or news on your phone. The purpose of this reflection is to put yourself squarely back into life and take note of what's around you. Let's retrain your brain to observe and take notice of patterns and details we've likely overlooked.

Your assignment: Take this book to a café, a park bench, or the comfort of your backyard. You decide. Sit and observe for twenty minutes. Look and listen to what's around you. You'll catch so much when you really pay attention. What you find might be subtle, but if you are still and observe, you might notice something new. When your twenty minutes are up, use this page to write down your observations, along with any feelings or emotions you may have noticed arise. If you noticed anything that sparked an idea or thought, write it here. Enjoy

CHAPTER 2

NURTURING CREATIVITY

It seems the way we currently nurture (or don't nurture) creativity is flawed. In homes where kids have parental support, they grow up confident. Once they go to school, they begin to feel the soft blow of judgment based on correct or incorrect answers. Out-of-the-box idea generation can gently sway toward quiet conformity to meet the expectations necessary to ace the test.

This is the beginning of the end of divergent thinking for many kids who are hungry to achieve academic excellence. Divergent thinking is the generation of a variety of ideas and alternative solutions to problems (Bertagnoli 2022). It is the kind of thinking that leads to generating ideas and solving problems, contrasting with convergent thinking which typically leads to the "correct" answers or solutions rather than original ones.

Rewarded by privileges that accompany achievement, such as invitation for enrichment opportunities and serving as exemplary behavior for others, good grades, and the value of earning them by producing expected results, helps to squelch the inner voice of inspiration.

"Divergent thinking is the ability to generate alternatives," said Spencer Harrison, associate professor of organizational behavior at a management school. Divergent thinkers question the status quo. They reject "we've always done it this way" as a reason, he said (Bertagnoli 2022).

Traditional exams test the student's ability to memorize and regurgitate information with limited freedom for interpreting. In that sense, a part of the creative mind is put on hold in favor of conformity to what is expected and rewarded. It's not to say that subjects with clear-cut answers, such as math and science, should not be memorized or tested—they should—just that our emphasis on correct and perfection as a standard at a young age requires consideration.

Our attempt to quantify a student's performance through standardized tests is beginning to be met with some resistance and begs the question, are these tests the correct vehicle to access learning? With students under increasing degrees of pressure to do well that their physical health is impacted, the increasing number of tests to measure both student and teacher success may be hitting overload (Kaufman 2012). The old adage "let kids be kids" is being pushed aside. Younger and younger kids are feeling the pressure, from grades to social media to youth sports that are taking the fun out of play.

Play, a critical aspect of childhood, is being replaced with intensity, judgment, and structure. It's enough to take the wind off anyone's sails, let alone a child's. "Research has shown a strong link between creative play and physical, cognitive, language, and social development. But recently, academic readiness has led the teachers to focus more on structured activities that are designed to promote academic results and help the students pass the test. This focus has led to a decrease in playful learning" (Teaching Through Play 2019).

The first psychologist to study cognitive development was Jean Piaget. He believed children learn about the world around them by making observations and being an active participant to build, adapt, and gain knowledge. This, in turn, helps children develop what he called "schemes" in cognitive development, which are "building blocks of cognitive models and help us to form a mental representation of the world around us." Through play, new information is acquired, and children learn if what they are experiencing fits in with the schemes they have developed. Lev Vygotsky, a Russian psychologist, believed social interaction plays a critical role in children's learning and is a continuous process that is influenced by culture. Best known for his socio-cultural theory, his theory included imitation, guided learning, and collaborative learning as key factors (Cherry 2022). One of Vygotsky's well-known concepts was the zone of proximal development. This is essentially the gap between what a child does and does not know. Acquiring the missing information requires skills that a child does not yet possess or cannot use independently but can with the help of what he referred to as a "more knowledgeable other," or a person who has greater knowledge and skills than the learner. This and his sociocultural theory highlight the importance of interaction between individuals and society in human development.

What impact does this have on curiosity, creativity, imagination, and exploration? What impact does this have on mental fitness in a post-COVID-19 world? What impact does this have on pursuing dreams verses doing what's expected?

What impact does this have on leadership in the workplace or contributing to effective teams?

RELEARNING CREATIVITY

The present model of our education system is more like a factory, where children are on a path focused on achievement beginning at a young age. I see with my own children, more emphasis on being correct and less on the freedom to imagine. Since I was the kid who liked to think outside the box, it was always a challenge to conform to the rules and expectations of traditional education. My mind was not adept at focusing on the slim details or regurgitating memorized and monotonous content for the sake of getting a decent grade. It took quelling my imagination to focus and do what was expected. I'm quite certain that's what contributed to my intentional abandonment of my creative self—to become what was expected.

From standardized tests, state requirements, and a one-size-fits-all curriculum, it shouldn't be surprising there's less creativity in the classroom. Fostering passion, curiosity, imagination, exploration, and problem-solving is not earning the attention in the classroom that our children need to cultivate their creativity. This is less the fault of the educators and more the antiquated framework of the historical education system founded in Europe in the late eighteenth century and adopted in North America during the mid-nineteenth century. Then there was the No Child Left Behind (NCLB) act for K–12 general education in the United States from 2002 to 2015. The law was controversial for its requirement to hold schools accountable for how kids learned and achieved, which would result in a penalty (University of Minnesota 2022).

Creativity, unlike innovation, is a distinctively human quality and even among humans remains a mystery to many who don't feel they possess this trait.

To many people, finding the magic sauce necessary to develop creativity within the self is a mystery, as it's viewed as a slippery and nebulous concept.

"In May 2013, *TIME* magazine published the results of a poll that found 94 percent of Americans value creativity in others, more than they value intelligence, compassion, humor, ambition, or beauty. In 2012, for the second year running, the adjective most used by members of LinkedIn to describe themselves is 'creative.' The occurrence of the word *creative* and *creativity* in books in American English from 1800-2008 suggests that both words became popularized in the twentieth century, after World War 2" (Haberski 2013). One interpretation as to why this might be the case is that there is a correlation between the rise of the use of this word and the need for human creativity as a factor of our society in general and with the economy specifically.

WHY IMAGINATION AND PLAY MATTER AT A YOUNG AGE

Creativity and problem-solving are basic skills required to deal with problems, whether at home or work. Coming up with ideas uses one's imagination to see things differently. Play is the vehicle that offers opportunities for imagination. Imagination fosters cognitive and social development, which is why playing when children are young and in early childhood education is so critical. Imagination is the door to possibilities, as it's how children learn critical thinking and creative problem-solving skills while learning about the world, like when preschoolers are provided with opportunities to solve problems, such as zipping a jacket or pulling on a sock, for example.

It is understood that there is a link between play and creativity. Specifically, both are linked to divergent thinking, which is about generating multiple creative solutions to the same problem. Play has been found to aid in the development of divergent thinking and, therefore, would be an important component of creative problem-solving.

Convergent thinking is a process of figuring out a concrete solution to any problem associated with speed, accuracy, and logic, whereas divergent thinking is non-linear and associated with spontaneity and is more free-flowing. While both types are similar to some extent, our schools and universities tend to prioritize a convergent type of thinking.

What we see today—age- and ability-based classrooms with a focus on students producing results through memorization and testing— reinforces and rewards a robotic and one-size-fits-all approach. Through various state-based initiatives, schools have attempted to incorporate opportunities for students to discover their passion and reduce the unnecessary rote memorization and standardized testing. Creativity and innovation can be hard to measure.

One learning method that has integrated an opportunity for kids to develop their creative passion is the Waldorf method of education. Its founder, Rudolf Steiner, wanted to create a holistic education system that could nurture a child through experiential learning and a passion for learning (2015). Art-themed recreation, along with practical skills like baking or gardening, help students foster collaborative environments and curious minds. The curriculum is focused on creative learning over academics. Developing emotionally, physically, and intellectually in mixed-age classrooms without the use of any digital resources and instead and emphasis on creativity is the focus.

Another method to note is the Montessori method. It was developed by an Italian physician, Dr. Maria Montessori, in the early 1900s (Jones 2022). Her approach was to foster a self-directed educational experience for children toward active and independent learning. The Montessori method places a high value on "children's work" through play and curiosity and dismisses standardized tests and grades.

The bottom line is that by allowing kids to discover their internal paths of interest, explore their passions, use their imaginations, and develop creative solutions to their problems, we can set them up to thrive and change the world.

In the very early school years, everything is new and exciting, and children are allowed to explore life, have fun, and socialize, but soon that passion gets squashed when we remove parts of the curriculum that foster creativity and keep the doors of imagination open. It's the free flow of creativity that lays the path for potential future entrepreneurship.

NURTURING CREATIVITY AS ADULTS

While the education system is certainly a big part of that puzzle, you can, as an adult, still grow and discover in a magical way if you're ready to make a difference in your life, or if you're a parent, to make a difference in the life of your child.

Real life is complex and imprecise. Creativity in the workplace is vital. Yet, when you think of a creative space, like an art studio for example, that is the opposite of what you'll encounter in the workplace. In a study conducted by Adobe (the graphics software company), it was found that 75 percent of the respondents felt they were not living up to their creative potential (Adobe 2020), while another study conducted by Fast Company found that 60 percent of CEOs say creativity is the most important skill for an employee. An IBM survey of 1,500 top executives in sixty countries picked it as the most desirable CEO quality. Companies are recognizing that, when employees are allowed to be more creative, the company benefits (Carr 2010). Just as when students are given choice in the classroom, which is empowering and allows for higher academic achievement, employees who are allowed to incorporate more creativity into their role can also attain strong results in the workplace.

Creativity is useful for any job, especially when applied to problem-solving.

First, it's important to stop thinking of creativity as something associated only with the visual or performing arts. Creativity is useful for any job, especially when applied to problem-solving.

Second, creativity in the workplace is not about just making things look good, but rather it is about creative thinking and creative problem-solving, collaboration, and team efficiency. The study of creativity on an individual level, among social groups at work, across cultures, and in broader political systems has generated a deeper understanding of the value, impact, and process for harnessing this mysterious quality.

Third, creativity can be conceptualized as both a process and an outcome. There's no one-size-fits all definition. Three interdependent capabilities essential to our own well-being, as well as to the well-being of society, is an understanding of creativity, innovation, and design. Some benefits of inter-dependence on creativity are better teams. Interdependence is one of the six principles required for building high-performance organizations, the principle that builds cooperation in the workplace in order for your work culture to thrive, and the universal collaborative principle that grows and develops from a sense of community and the spirit of employee support.

KEY
TAKEAWAYS
Chapter2

- Creativity and problem-solving are basic skills required to deal with problems, whether at home or work.

- Play is the vehicle that offers opportunities for imagination.

- Imagination is the door to the possibility of identifying and creatively solving the problems around us.

- Play gets a bad rep... In our work-obsessed society, it is often viewed as silly, unproductive, or time-consuming. This is why many adults tend to let go of their inner child, focusing instead on the responsibilities and priorities of adulthood.

- Play is just as important for adults as it is for children. For kids, it develops cognitive, emotional and behavioral skills. In adults, it is an investment in self-care and helps relax, recharge and reconnect with the world around us. This in turn, brings joy to life, helps relieve stress, boosts mental and physical well-being.

- Creativity is NOT something only associated only with the visual or performing arts. It is useful in all aspects of life; personal or professional.

What can you do?

- Get out and get social! I'm not always a fan of being in large groups, so for me, being social means connecting in smaller groups. The key is that you regularly connect and build meaningful relationships.

- Find a pastime our of pure enjoyment rather than a necessity or obligation. Pursuing a hobby or interest helps you to learn more about yourself and helps find meaning in life.

When trying to think of new ideas or solutions to problems, it's tempting to stick with the very first suggestions. However, the first ideas may not always be the best. For this reflection, I'd like to introduce you to what's called the Concept Fan. Created by Edward de Bono (Visual Paradigm 2022), this technique develops the principle of "taking a step back" to get a broader viewpoint. The Concept Fan is a great tool to use for widening the search for solutions when you have rejected all obvious alternatives. Give it a try!

1. Draw a circle below, just right of center.

2. Write the problem you are trying to solve in it.

3. To the right of the circle, draw three lines (connected to the circle like sun rays). Each line represents a possible solution to the problem. So now identify and write a possible solution on each of the three lines. This is a starting point for your ideas.

4. If this does not give you the idea you are looking for, then repeat the process by redefining the problem more broadly. Write this broader definition in a circle to the left of the first one.

5. Draw an arrow from the initial problem definition to the new one to show the linkage between the problems. Then radiate possible solutions from this broader definition.

6. Keep repeating the process, reframing problem state-ments, and fanning out ideas.

Additional Space to Explore

More space to reflect!

CHAPTER 3

MINDFULNESS

We are all familiar with the clutter of unending emails, meetings, and to-do lists that liter busy workweeks and jumble the mind. Add social media usage in the mix and working from home, and you have a recipe for anxiety, lack of focus, and depression. Studies show that excessive social media use and exacerbated mental health issues correlate in several ways. One study, published in the Canadian Journal of Psychiatry, indicates that higher screen time directly correlates with higher anxiety levels (Boers, Afzali, and Conrad 2020). We are constantly being pulled in different directions, and our collective mental health is suffering as a result.

Creativity is like a spark that ignites your soul into an awakened state, inspiring you to go beyond, go deeper, and pull from the most inner depths of your being.

It seems obvious to me now that in order to embrace this spark, cultivate creative experiences, and find creative inspiration, we need to be much more acutely aware of our environment. That is, we need to be more mindful of what's going on around us so we can easily identify the patterns that can inspire or the puzzle pieces that don't fit together and oppose the patterns we see around us. If we're constantly involved in our routine, unaware of the new things around us, we will lack inspiration. When you have multiple interests beyond, say, your work, you have additional touch points for finding and cultivating creative and inspirational opportunities through mindfulness. Just being aware and feeling that moment when things connect and switches the light bulb on.

THE VALUE MINDFULNESS HAS ON CREATIVITY

Once you understand the value and impact mindfulness has on creativity, it's time to get a little deeper. You're probably familiar with the notion of a lightbulb people speak of when sharing how an idea popped into their head unexpectedly. When you aren't tuned into the moment, those lightbulbs won't create sparks to get your attention. Why is it, then, that oftentimes good ideas come when you're driving or doing something completely unrelated to that idea?

You engage many parts of your brain during the creative process. According to Kaufman, the executive function network "is active when you're concentrating on a challenging lecture or engaging in complex problem-solving and reasoning that puts heavy demands on working memory."

The key to cultivating mindfulness that promotes creativity as opposed to reducing it is choosing a method that allows your mind to wander and encourages curiosity. There are meditation styles that can be used for this purpose. Open monitoring meditation is one such method that increases the ability to generate new ideas (Colzato, Szapora, Lippelt, and Hommel 2014).

Open monitoring meditation, or "open awareness" or "choice-less awareness," requires nothing but your thoughts, so it's easy for beginners and advanced meditators alike. It really couldn't be easier. All it requires is that you simply allow thoughts to come and go through your mind, just noticing them, and letting them go. "It might seem passive, and it is sometimes called a 'lazy person's meditation,' but it can be surprisingly hard not to focus on something, and even experienced meditators will still find themselves engaging with their thoughts." So you are aware of thoughts but not doing anything to prompt or manipulate them (Bloomsoup 2021).

Reduced stress, increased happiness, and better overall mental health are just three benefits associated with meditation. Open monitoring meditation has been specifically linked to increased memory, productivity, and self-awareness, as well as improved creativity. This may be the result of a heightened ability to make connections and think laterally, as meditation encourages a more equally engaged brain.

Creativity is not exactly a simple process, according to researcher Scott Barry Kaufman, PhD. He sees it as "messy," and writes, "The creative process—from the first drop of paint on the canvas to the art exhibition—involves a mix of emotions, drives, skills, and behaviors" (Kaufman 2014).

In Allen Gannett's book *The Creative Curve,* he sought to uncover what the world's most successful people did to reveal their own creative brilliance. What he found was that this notion of the lightbulb is a myth. Successful people, according to his research, followed four patterns that increased their chances. Most of the innovators he interviewed were able to intuitively balance an idea between being familiar verses novel. Gannett attributes this balance to their mainstream success as they know their audience, what they want, and how to make subtle changes while still maintaining audience interest. This is what he called the "creative curve" (Gannett 2018).

Whether you're seeking to enhance your creativity, or to find solutions to problems in a new and innovative way, in my view, there's a connection and an order to how one should address and proceed.

The creative process model has traditionally been broken down into the following five stages of creativity: preparation, incubation, insight, evaluation, and elaboration (occasionally the names can vary).

Creativity seeks to inspire an idea, while innovation takes that idea and applies it to solving a problem.

There is a distinct order to these. Creativity would come first, and innovation might follow. It's worth noting there's no guarantee innovation will follow, but the hope is it might.

The creative problem-solving process, meanwhile, includes the following steps:

Step 1. Identify the goal, wish, or challenge.

Step 2. Gather data.

Step 3. Clarify the problem.

Step 4. Generate ideas.

Step 5. Develop solutions.

Step 6. Plan for action (Advertising Row 2021).

Meanwhile, the innovation process typically consists of the following stages:

- Discovery

- Development

- Commercialization or idea-generation and mobilization

- Advocacy and screening

- Experimentation

- Commercialization

- Diffusion and implementation

All of these processes have truth and value, but if you're looking to tap into innovation, it likely comes from a place that's a combination of these processes mixed with a little more work upfront before you even get started.

While these are helpful steps and tools, they fail to look at an individual's subtle and nuanced life experience that might interfere or prevent a person from realizing, actualizing, or optimizing the opportunity to contribute. As indicated above, regarding the lightbulb idea of creativity, if a person sees accessing a novel idea as limited only to a select few people, then depending on their willingness to put themselves out there, there's a chance they could just disregard creativity as something they don't have. Their reason for dismissing their abilities might come from several factors, including confidence, degree of exposure to creativity during childhood, parental or teacher encouragement, or self-criticism. That's why a deeper dive is necessary as a prelude to any of these steps to make them actually work. This is the front-end work that needs to be done first. The front-end work establishes confidence and, in turn, gives you permission to set your creative self free to fly into new uncharted seas.

DIVING DEEP: HEADFIRST INTO THE CREATIVE PROCESS

In the creative process, step 1 is preparation. This is viewed as a deep dive, but it isn't deep enough. Preparation by most definitions of the creative process refers to the research or exploration a person does on a given topic prior to embarking on the creative journey. This might mean different things to different people, but the gist of it is to explore something of interest you want to learn more about or find inspiration from to generate ideas or get those creative juices flowing.

Here's where I have an issue. While some people who are familiar with the creative process might be able to go from seeking inspiration to a lightbulb moment, many people don't get past preparing. My question is, why not? One might say not everyone is creative, but I would disagree. Humans are innately creative, able to identify problems, and find solutions.

Many people feel stifled by the challenge of finding inspiration, but their failure to launch can't be blamed on missing a step in the process. This is where the deeper dive is necessary to inspire inspiration.

First and foremost, give yourself permission to be creative. You may not be able to draw a stick figure, but that's okay. Creativity comes in many forms, and you start to become creative when you own it.

GET OUTSIDE TO FIND MINDFULNESS AND INSPIRATION

Next, it's important to adopt a practice of mindfulness and awareness. By this, I don't mean always bringing yourself into the present. I mean paying attention to the world around you, embracing, and reflecting. Live like you are a live antenna and can feel all your senses. They've been dulled by our digital fog, so becoming mindful is being alive.

The qualities I associate with activity are daydreaming, trust of self, willingness to embrace vulnerability, an openness to unknown and unexpected, a little rebelliousness, inspiration informed by recognition of patterns, and listening to the nudge and pull to create, followed by evaluation and willingness to fail.

It's not a means to an end, and it's not a guarantee, but it will give you the best chance of success.

Why are there people who have great ideas they can't bring to fruition or artists not showing their incredible talents? Did they miss a step in one of these processes, or did the steps overlook an important element—the individual variations promoted by subjective experience or environment?

Giving yourself permission is part of living well and being authentic to yourself. Author Elizabeth Gilbert defines it as a higher vocation of living. She encourages people not to waste their talents because we have such a short duration of time here on this planet and our mortality is precious, so we need to work to quell that panic to turn it into something inspiring and be as creative as possible. Pathologies you don't want to go to the grave with, like shame and suffering, can be healed through creativity. People who create art see their commitment as suffering or they're not doing it right, but using their suffering as a badge or validation they are a serious artist is incorrect. Gilbert sees art as having to do not with suffering but with pleasure. Art provides ways to access collaboration with divine inspiration, not wrestle with it but work with it and respect it in partnership to be embraced. She suggests allowing yourself the freedom to be curious to find your passion while enjoying the process and trusting the pleasure of creating (Gilbert 2009).

In the book *The Art of Innovation* by Tom Kelley, he comments on the belief that creative individuals are few and far between. As well as people and companies searching for novel solutions, he recognizes that creativity sells. Tom Kelley is the bestselling author of *Creative Confidence*, *The Art of Innovation*, and *The Ten Faces of Innovation*, as well as a partner at the renowned design and innovation consultancy IDEO. "We all have a creative side, and it can flourish if you spawn a culture to encourage it, one that embraces risks and wild ideas and tolerates the occasional failure" (Kelley 2001).

In Kelley's view, inspiration comes from being close to the action, businesses that foster a culture of creativity through fun, an openness to the world around, an acceptance of failure, risk diving into the unknown, and adopting a nimble and agile mindset that accepts coloring outside the lines but can evaluate when it's not too far outside the lines too. Inspiration comes from organizations who adopt this mindset and position themselves to inspire creativity and drive innovation.

In the end, whether you believe the spark of an idea is divinely inspired or a result of neurological processes, they are likely all contributing to the outcome, but an individual must, at some point, be open and willing to allow being part of the process first.

KEY
TAKEAWAYS
Chapter 3

- Distractions such as social media, unending busyness, meetings and to-do lists contribute to anxiety and lack of focus. This in turn creates a reactionary "get it done to survive" mindset, removing the joy and hindering creativity.

- Inspiration comes from being open to the world around us.

- Meditation encourages a more fully engaged brain. Reduced stress, increased happiness, and better overall mental health are just three benefits associated with meditation.

- Live like you are a live antenna and can feel all your senses. They've been dulled by our digital fog, so becoming mindful is being alive.

- Our time on this planet is short. Everyone has a gift or talent they should not waste during this lifetime. Mindfulness helps you to access and tap into your hidden talents and find inspiration. The only prerequisite to accessing your gifts is a willingness to try something new.

- Creativity, like a garden needs time and energy to grow. Mindfulness and meditation are a key ingredient in the recipe.

What can you do?

- Try to adopt the traveler mindset in your daily life. Pay closer attention to the details of your surroundings, as if you're visiting a new city.

- Be curious as you explore your world. Meet people, ask questions and listen.

- Give yourself permission to try new things. If you were on trip, wouldn't you want to try a new cuisine or experience the culture? Bring that attitude to your daily life.

In the process of researching this book, I stumbled upon the following "New Year Prayer: 7 Reflection Points for Wholeness and Well-Being," by Lisa Lochhead, an artist from the UK. Take a moment to read her words, then reflect on your own personal goal for today and how it fits into your vision for your future. In the space below, write your own small prayer to the universe.

May Self-Acceptance fuel your actions and decisions—so you walk tenderly and at One within your own Heart

May Courage hold your hand—As the Light of Love illumes the ripeness in learnings, insights, challenges, and changes in the year ahead.

May Love's Pulse be known to you and soothe any places of tiredness and fatigue as you walk the Way of Being.

May Creativity show you the way in service to your higher purpose and potentiality—planting seeds in rich, fertile soil.

May Communion teach you that you are not alone as you tread the path into a deeper Aloneness.

May true Friendship be in your life. One or two in shared intimacy and openness of Being are precious gems in a world addicted to false belonging.

May Belonging be your Real Home. Where you can find rest in the unrested, comfort in the uncomfortable, peace in the sorrow, life in death.

Additional Space to Reflect

More space...Yay!

_____
_____
_____
_____
_____
_____
_____
_____
_____
_____
_____
_____
_____
_____
_____
_____
_____
_____
_____
_____
_____
_____
_____
_____
_____
_____
_____
_____
_____
_____
_____
_____

CHAPTER 4

DAYDREAMING

We are the architects of our own lives.

But with the constant bombarding of stimuli from every facet of our lives, our creativity can suffer. When you realize the benefits of creativity, you begin to recognize the factors that increase this magic sauce in your life. Daydreaming is one of those. Daydreaming increases creativity, happiness, and mental health. If you're super connected digitally (overly busy), you may be disconnecting from your inner creative self. Being wrapped up in the external world of work and life prevents us from accessing our inner world. It's this inner personal world where dreams, hopes, and our true emotional and authentic self come to life. That's why we tend to feel less anxious and depressed when we tap into our inner being.

The tricky part is making the time for regular unfocused thinking. Unfocused cerebral activity deepens creativity as it encourages the unconscious mind to release material in the form of ideas, inspirations, and memories that bubble up from a deep place that might not have come to the surface (Fink et. al 2009, 734-48). The key is that in order to open what's in the depths of our subconscious, we need to let go, not do. To just be and take a mental vacation.

With your mind free, you'll feel better, see possibilities, and uncover solutions. That's why daydreaming can serve as a motivator, helping people work toward their goal. For example, if a person daydreams about rising to the top at work, visualizing themself in that role, and processing how to get there, the daydream can serve as a motivator.

There is a difference between mind wandering and daydreaming. Mind wandering is less intensive, easy to fall into but also easy to come out of because there's less depth to the thoughts. With adaptive (normal) daydreaming, it takes a little bit more effort to regain awareness from the level of thinking you're engaged in. Meaning, you're a little more absorbed in a daydream than you are when you just let your mind wander (Stop Maladaptive Daydreaming 2022).

Daydreaming opens us up to discover our authentic selves or inner "truth." It realizes the real us and encourages growth provided we allow our daydreams to take us to places both pleasurable and uncomfortable. It can produce deep emotions, and as a result it will strengthen our identity and foster awareness that helps us grow.

As I mentioned earlier in this book, I've always been a daydreamer. Sadly, I observed something during my childhood that continues to be true for adults as well: daydreaming gets a bad rep! Yet mind wandering provides a way for the brain to process self-related information to update our life story. Imagining the stories in our daydreams helps us to make sense of who we are and provides us with the tools to build our narrative identity. It's not a bad thing. It's a necessary part of human development.

In my own life, I can say daydreaming has had a positive impact on my problem-solving and idea-generation abilities. When I've had too much of a given task and know I'm in need of a break, it's not unusual for me to put on my earbuds filled with instrumental music and allow my mind to wander and my body to be still. I wouldn't call this meditation but a mental break. It's during this state of relaxation and pause when sometimes I catch an idea or a solution to a problem that had been on my mind. It's as if the break opened up a new set of opportunities. I encourage you to give it a try.

A wandering mind—another term used to refer to daydreaming—is something we all do every few minutes. In fact, studies say about 25 to 50 percent of our waking hours are spent with our mind wandering. One moment, we are at work or on a Zoom call; the next, we are imagining ourselves on a vacation in a tropical destination. One cause for the bad reputation daydreaming gets is likely attributed to the belief it hinders productivity or serves as an enemy to one's ability to focus and concentrate. While there may be some truth in that, it turns out there are several kinds of mind wandering. Some kinds do, in fact, make you more unhappy or unproductive; however, the key is that not all do. One can learn techniques to control a wandering mind and achieve better concentration and fun. In fact, with the right tools, daydreaming can be more of a super tool in our mental arsenal that will even serve to motivate us. Daydreaming as a source of creative inspiration seems logical, but the jury is still out on research results that prove a conclusive correlation between daydreaming and creative inspiration.

In fact, with the right tools, daydreaming can be more of a super tool in your mental arsenal that will even serve to motivate you.

Mind wandering may go hand in hand with more frequent eye blinking, research suggests. In a study published in 2010 in the journal Psychological Science, researchers asked people to read a passage from a book and tracked their eye movements as they read. They found that participants blinked more during the moments when their minds wandered, compared with the moments in which they were more focused on the task (Association for Psychological Science 2010).

PRODUCTIVE DAYDREAMING

If your routine daydreams involve remembering to take out the trash or get things done on your endless task list, your creativity may not be impacted. Studies have shown there are different types of daydreams people have and that not all equally impact inspiration and creativity. This is where learning more effective daydreaming might inspire more creative inspiration. If nothing else, it shows that daydreaming isn't necessarily bad (Zedelius 2020).

THE BENEFITS OF DAYDREAMING

Another perspective worth noting is, given our hyper plugged-in culture, we may be limited in our time truly connecting to ourselves. We are inundated with endless emails, posts, and texts to the extent that we don't allow ourselves time to just be. Allowing time and freedom to daydream permits our spontaneous selves to reappear and is said to reduce anxiety and depression. The key is to allow undirected thinking as opposed to directed thinking; hence, a good dose of mind wandering. This may help you tap into creative potential and feel better about living. The unfocused allows thoughts and ideas to creep up from the deeper mind: the unconscious. When we allow our ideas to marinate in our unconscious mind, to bubble up in the form of a daydream, we open to the possibility of thinking of new solutions and possibilities, even when we aren't directly working on tasks or problems.

"People with efficient brains may have too much brain capacity to stop their minds from wandering," Eric Schumacher, an associate professor at the Georgia Institute of Technology, explained in a statement. In other words, there's power in daydreaming after all. This makes a nice change from older studies that have associated frequent mind wandering with lower scores on memory tests, high school exams, and reading comprehension (Georgia Institute of Technology 2017).

Participants of a study by Schumacher and colleagues monitored the brain activity of volunteers who were asked to concentrate on a stationary point for five minutes. From this, they were able to establish which areas of the brain work together when the body is in an awake resting state. Next, a series of tests were introduced to measure intellectual capacity and creativity, along with a person's tendency to daydream in normal life as well as MRI scans to access brain systems. This, in turn, provided a correlation between those who demonstrated more intellectual capacity and their less intellectual or creative counterparts. This demonstrates that higher brain efficiency enables the individual more room to think and therefore making routine tasks easier and increasing the opportunity for daydreaming. Another example of this is how easily a person can tune in or out of a given task without missing a beat.

"Our findings remind me of the absent-minded professor—someone who's brilliant but off in his or her own world, sometimes oblivious to their own surroundings," Schumacher said. "Or school children who are too intellectually advanced for their classes. While it may take five minutes for their friends to learn something new, they figure it out in a minute, then check out and start daydreaming."

Daydreaming, as luck would have it, is one way. Undirected thinking may lead to concrete, creative results while daydreaming inspires intangible forms of creativity that can benefit both work and life in general. Daydreams can give rise to an innovative approach to problems that lead to useful ideas and lifted moods. Jonah Lehrer, author of *Imagine: How Creativity Works*, is also an advocate of daydreaming (Lehrer 2012).

Creativity is a gift, and it needs to be fed in order to produce more. Daydreaming is fun, so use it to spark more of what will make you happy. Remove yourself from your busyness and external stimuli every day and take a vacation to see what's there. You might be pleasantly surprised by what you find and what results.

It's worth noting that "if you were to never let your mind wander, you would have to reside in either one of two states: perfect awareness, in which your mind is empty, or perfect focus on whatever thing you're currently doing. The term maladaptive daydreaming is an intensified degree of the level of thinking and frequency of daydreaming. The degree that one should allow themselves to daydream is entirely subjective. If it's actively impacting or interfering your real life (e.g., causing an inability to concentrate, interfering with school or work, et cetera), you may be dealing with maladaptive daydreaming, in which case, you may want to adopt one of several available techniques to help people who struggle with daydreaming too frequently to ensure that it doesn't happen as often" (Stop Maladaptive Daydreaming 2022).

So, if you've been told to get your head out of the clouds, maybe it's time to accept it as a compliment.

KEY TAKEAWAYS
Chapter 4

- Daydreaming increases creativity, happiness, and mental health.

- Being super connected digitally (overly busy), you may be disconnecting from your inner creative self. Same with being wrapped up in the external world of work and life, it prevents us from accessing our inner world.

- The inner personal world is where dreams, hopes, and our true emotional and authentic self come to life.

- Tapping into our inner being, can help feel less anxious and depressed. Daydreaming opens us up to discover our authentic selves or inner "truth."

- When we allow our daydreams to take us to places both pleasurable and uncomfortable, we strengthen our identity and foster awareness that helps us grow.

- Undirected thinking may lead to concrete, creative results while daydreaming inspires intangible forms of creativity that can benefit both work and life in general.

What can you do?

Remove yourself from your busyness and external stimuli every day and take a vacation to see what's there.

Make it a ritual to put aside 5 minutes to just daydream. One way might be to put aside 5 minutes either just after you wake up or just before bed. Sit and imagine your dreams. I mean, what is it that you really want? Imagine it with your whole being so that you can keep this little dream nugget in your mind throughout your day without even realizing it. This will help motivate you toward accomplishing your dreams.

Daydreaming is an effective way to engage your imagi-nation for both inspiration and creative problem-solving. Find a quiet space and get comfortable. Daydreaming about achieving your goals can also help motivate you to pursue them. It's time to give yourself permission to let your mind wander. You'll be amazed at how creative you can be. Mute or turn your phone off. You may want to set a timer for ten minutes. Let your mind wander. When the alarm goes off, write down some of the thoughts that wandered in your mind during this daydream session.

Next time you have a few free minutes to spend, consider daydreaming instead of surfing around online. You'll feel more relaxed, positive, and motivated as a result.

CHAPTER 5

OBSTACLES

Have you ever felt a judging eye from a parent? Say, perhaps, you were on the way out one night, and one of them asked, "Is that what you're wearing?" At that moment, you probably felt deflated and wondered, *Why, does it look bad?* Would you rush back to your room and change or wear what you intended? Now go back to when you were even younger. Let's say in elementary school, there was a time when you asked an unexpected question or shared what you thought was a brilliant insight or creation and were made to feel like what you shared was not appropriate for the given time. Maybe the teacher inadvertently squelched your enthusiasm by suggesting your feedback wasn't welcomed at that time.

In my house, I would often have crazy ideas I'd share with my father. As a natural entrepreneur, I was constantly concocting scenarios where I was convinced I might have a stellar successful idea. I'd get excited about telling my father, and he would always reply with what was a perfectly logical explanation of why my idea was not feasible. I know he didn't mean to bury my creativity, but the result was a sense of rejection. As a parent, it's hard to listen to crazy ideas when you're busy or think you have all the answers. I'm not suggesting the everyone-gets-a-trophy approach to handling a child's nonsensical ideas, but I feel we would serve our children well as teachers and parents if we welcome their crazy ideas. Welcome the ideas that might make you laugh but make your child beam with pride. Welcome the ideas that are so over the top from reality that only a miracle could make them happen. Welcome all those crazy ideas. We need to embrace them so when our kids get older, they, too, can respect their crazy and see where it goes. If it's possible to be both open to crazy ideas while wading in a pool of logic and reality, that's what we should be, encouraging creativity and fostering a person's permission to create, be curious, and contribute rather than feeling rejected and judged.

What I'm trying to say can be summed up by Apple's 1984 Think Different campaign:

"Here's to the crazy ones. The misfits. The rebels. The trouble-makers. The round pegs in the square holes. The ones who see things differently. They're not fond of rules. And they have no respect for the status quo. You can quote them, disagree with them, glorify or vilify them. About the only thing you can't do is ignore them. Because they change things. They push the human race forward. And while some may see them as the crazy ones, we see genius because the people who are crazy enough to think they can change the world are the ones who do" (Siltanen 2011).

As emotional beings, we seek out experiences that make us feel good and reinforce our value. If we fear our contribution is frivolous, unrealistic, outlandish, or guilty of wasting someone's time to share it, we would likely hold ourselves back from con-tributing. Nobody likes to feel like they're imposing or creating a burden. But if, when you were in elementary school, your curiosity was met with scornful judgments that made the words "creativity" or "imagination" feel negative, wouldn't you begin to push down those moments of curiosity in favor of conforming to expected norms and standards? As the focus of education lies in achievement versus creative expression and play, or as elementary schools reinforce rigidity and seriousness through less play and creativity, we are teaching our youth the rewards are for those who adhere and achieve. We are saying that thinking outside the box is great in theory but really not welcomed, and that we can say we welcome diversity of thoughts, but what we reward is uniformity. Having said that, there is no perfect educational model, but some are better than others. Depending on the teaching style used, some will minimize the child's ability to be creative while others will help it to flourish. Subjects like math, science, and history seem to require more structured answers, while other subjects might increase creativity in young children. Engaging the learner through collaboration with peers (cooperative learning) allows for creativity and an increase in achievement.

According to research conducted by Kyung Hee Kim, professor of education at the College of William and Mary, all aspects of student creativity at the K-12 level have been in significant decline for the last few decades. Based on scores from the Torrance Tests of Creative Thinking, her study reveals "that children have become less emotionally expressive, less energetic, less talkative and verbally expressive, less humorous, less imaginative, less unconventional, less lively and passionate, less perceptive, less apt to connect seemingly irrelevant things, less synthesizing, and less likely to see things from a different angle" (Kim 2011).

In speaking with teacher friends, they feel there isn't a lot of time for "fun," creative activities, and lessons anymore, even in elementary schools. Why? Because teachers are expected to "stick to the pacing guide," not veer off schedule, or they'll be behind the rest of the grade level. On top of that, teachers have few opportunities to be creative in their own methods or with materials because they must adhere to a prescribed curriculum directly from the teacher's guide or pre-written curriculum. Why is this? States are bound to the Common Core Standards. In the state of New York, CCS are now becoming the Next Generation Standards. The US really needs to look at the education successes in other countries and replicate those models (Education Northwest 2010).

The term "imposter syndrome" was first identified in 1978 by psychologists Pauline Rose Clance and Suzanne Imes. It is defined as a feeling of inadequacy that persists despite evident success (Yun 2018). People with imposter syndrome exhibit feelings of chronic self-doubt and the feeling of being a fraud. While imposter syndrome can affect anyone, a greater prevalence in high-achieving women has been found. Most experts believe that imposter syndrome is typically caused by cyclical societal norms and expectations. Severe self-doubt and some family dynamics from childhood can contribute to imposter syndrome as adults. This is a very common condition.

Failure Lab was founded in 2012, and according to their website, their mission is "to eliminate the fear of failure and encourage intelligent risk taking." Promoting the acceptance of failure serves to help create a comfort level and change the conversation about our views of success and our willingness to fail. The #ShareYourRejection hashtag on Twitter attempts to do the same thing. If we aren't afraid of failure and we accept that we are not a fraud, we can help to not only reduce the prevalence of imposter syndrome but use our experience with it as a transformative experience (Failure Lab 2021).

We are creatures of habit in search of pleasure and reward. Before we can create, we need to feel safe knowing we won't be rejected. We need to give ourselves permission to contribute, to laugh more, and find more joy, curiosity, and imagination. These are what fuels creativity and passion.

From Waldorf website:

- The goal of Waldorf education is to develop a student's ability to access his inner resources in order to transform both himself and the world around him. Founded in the early twentieth century and supported by contemporary brain research, Waldorf education seeks to nurture the whole child through experiential education that engages their imagination and their intellect, the right brain and their left brain, their body and their spirit. An emphasis on the arts develops a child's creativity and imagination and empowers them to become creative thinkers and problem-solvers in adulthood. A Waldorf educated student is prepared to encounter the challenges of the world around her with creativity, flexibility, and self-awareness.

- Our role as parents and teachers: As parents and teachers, it is our place to encourage creativity and teach our children to embrace it. It is our job to lead and guide by example—letting our kids discover, embrace, and change the world around them. It is not our job to take over or interrupt the natural process and love of learning. When we do this to children, it can inhibit the innate connections between kids, lead to a lack of trust, and, most of all—shuts creativity down. When parents and teachers step in too much, we send a message stating, "You're not capable, let me do it." As adults, we quickly forget the potential and remarkable miracles our children create. We cannot steal this opportunity away from them, as it leads not only to our children's loss but to our future losses as well. The future of entrepreneurship depends on us. It is our job to guide students. It is not our place to interfere with natural talents, abilities, and creativity that leads to creative genius (2015).

Social emotional learning (SEL) and growth mindset are two focus areas in education today. When these practices are implemented, learners become more self-aware and mindful of their social, emotional, and learning needs. Having that awareness can lead to greater creativity and achievement. People with a growth mindset believe talent and intelligence can grow with practice, effort, and experience.

FEELING LIKE AN IMPOSTER

I'm not sure when I first felt like a fraud, but I know the feeling of being inadequate followed me throughout my life. At different stages, there were different reasons I felt out of place and incomplete, like a hangnail that keeps getting caught on a garment, a painful reminder that creates a distorted distraction from reality.

As a child I was always a creative cyclone of energy. I was a terrible student with a speech impediment and a pile of crazy curly hair, but I could talk my way in or out of anything. This natural gift of gab provided cover for me to hide my true discomfort. It's easy to blend in when you're a good communicator, but it's difficult to be honest with yourself. Today, when I tell old friends I'm a social introvert, they laugh, unaware that I was uncomfortable in my skin.

When I changed my undergrad major from graphic design to communication on the advice from my father that there's no money to be made in art, I didn't know where I belonged. I wasn't one of the high-achieving girls, and teachers didn't take to mentor or guide me, so I was kind of lost. My parents certainly tried their best and meant well but didn't have high hopes for their untraditional kid.

I'm pretty sure I was labeled as the cute ditsy girl. I generally did what was expected and did little to outwardly express my creativity. On the contrary, I wanted to please and play safe, knowing I'd be judged as being too eccentric or trying to be "different" if I strayed from what might be a norm. At some point, I became my own worst enemy, hindering and sabotaging my own progress.

KEY
TAKEAWAYS
Chapter 5

- As parents or leaders, inviting ideas, listening without judgment and encouraging a freedom to explore is critical in cultivating a creative environment at home or work.

- If we fear our contribution is frivolous, unrealistic, outlandish, or guilty of wasting someone's time to share it, we would likely hold ourselves back from contributing

- Imposter Syndrome, a fear of inadequacy despite clear ability is real and can affect anyone. Placing less importance on societal norms and expectations can help minimize the self-doubt associated with fear of failure. This in turn will help prevent the fear of being a fraud.

- People have a need to belong and feel safe in knowing their ideas won't make them feel rejected.

- Doing what you "should" quiets your inner creative voice and can hinder you from becoming your true and authentic self.

This is the Obstacle Monster.

It gets in the way of finding your greatness.

The Obstacle Monster whispers negative thoughts like:
You're not worth it
Wait til later
What will people think?

Replace the negative thoughts with positive!

What can you do?

Act now, you're worth it!

Sometimes you need to step into the muck and take the messy path before you get to the intended destination.

When things get tough, it's usually because that something means a lot to you. It's those things that deserve your time and effort. Allow yourself to be vulnerable.

Life is not all rainbows and unicorns, but rolling your sleeves up and getting dirty is the first step.

How do you know you can't do something if you've never tried?

Take a moment to reflect on the things that hold you back from actualizing your dreams. In the column on the left, write down three things that prevent you from achieving your dreams. In the column on the right, write down three specific actions you will take to overcome those obstacles.

Perceived obstacles to achieving my dreams	Actions I will take to achieve my dreams

CREATIVE MINDSET

Wordnik defines mindset as a fixed mental attitude or disposition that predetermines a person's responses to and interpretations of situations. Wordnik also defines mindset as an inclination or a habit as a way of thinking and as an attitude or opinion, especially a habitual one (Wordnik 2009).

Having a creative mindset is really about opening up new ways of thinking to allow you to express your creativity, recognize inspiration, and view the world with a little more wonder and awe. According to Verywell Mind, "Your mindset is a set of beliefs that shape how you make sense of the world and yourself. It influences how you think, feel, and behave in any given situation. It means that what you believe about yourself impacts your success or failure" (Cherry 2022).

Stanford psychologist Carol Dweck discusses two main mindsets we can have in her book *Mindset: The New Psychology of Success*. She explains a fixed mindset and a growth mindset. Her research is on human motivation as she looks at why people succeed, or fail, and how mindset and beliefs play a role in what we want and whether we achieve it.

Dweck has found it is our mindsets that play a significant role in determining achievement and success.

As she describes it, "My work bridges developmental psychology, social psychology, and personality psychology, and examines the self-conceptions (or mindsets) people use to structure the self and guide their behavior. My research looks at the origins of these mindsets, their role in motivation and self-regulation, and their impact on achievement and interpersonal processes" (Dweck 2007).

A fixed mindset is when you believe your intelligence is fixed or your qualities are what you are born with and are not changeable. You would believe you're never going to be good at something if your mindset is fixed.

A growth mindset is whether you believe you can change and learn new abilities with effort, then your talents can be developed over time. This contributes to having a positive outlook about motivation and learning.

Additional benefits of a growth mindset include:

- Reduced burnout

- Fewer psychological problems, such as depression and anxiety

- Fewer behavioral problems

Herein lies the never-ending, age-old dilemma that remains the crux of the issue. How does one access their inner creative mindset at a moment's notice? In his 1996 book *Creativity: The Work and Lives of 91 Eminent People*, psychologist Mihaly Csikszentmihalyi suggested that "of all human activities, creativity comes closest to providing the fulfillment we all hope to get in our lives." He identified ten opposite traits that, when they interact in a complex manner, will positively increase one's creativity (Csikszentmihalyi 1996).

1. Energetic and focused

2. Smart and naive

3. Playful and disciplined

4. Realistic and imaginative

5. Extroverted and introverted

6. Proud and modest

7. Masculine and feminine

8. Conservative and rebellious

9. Passionate and objective

10. Sensitive and joyful

Not only is creativity a complex topic in and of itself, but there is no clear and concise definition of creativity. It is generally viewed as the tendency to solve problems or create new things in novel ways.

Here are a few rules I feel will help boost creative genus:

1. Be curious. The more you know, the better you are. The more you have a curious mind, the more resourceful you are. When you have a desire to learn more about a variety of things, you'll be able to draw upon a wide variety of knowledge and insights. This increases the chances that you'll make connections that spark ideas. Think like a sleuth with a desire to learn more. When you explore, you place yourself in the situation and weave yourself into whatever outcomes may result. You become invested. According to cognitive scientist and researcher Elizabeth Bonawitz, curiosity is innate in all humans—a sensation much like hunger or thirst. "Curiosity acts as a kind of filter you put over the world to help the mind decide what information to attend to," she says. "It's a physiological response that helps drive action and decision-making to support learning." Highlighting ambiguity sparks curiosity. Helping students recognize gaps in their current knowledge and getting children to generate predictions and engage their assumptions about the world are a few ways educators and parents create moments that generate a curious response (Boudreau 2020).

2. Adopt a playful attitude. Psychologists have long believed that intelligence plays a critical role in creativity. In Lewis Terman's famous longitudinal study of gifted children, researchers found that while high IQ was necessary for great creativity, not all people with high IQs are creative. Csikszentmihalyi believes that creative people must be smart, but they must be capable of looking at things in fresh, even naive, ways, playful in the discovery yet

disciplined in the pursuit and passionate. As Thomas Edison famously suggested, "Genius is 1 percent inspiration and 99 percent perspiration" (Csikszentmihalyi 1996).

3. Adopt a gratitude or mindfulness practice. When you build in time for a spiritual practice, you are surrendering to opening yourself up to receiving. This vulnerability and acceptance allow you to see, hear, and recognize those momentary sparks of genius. When you perceive the world with a fresh perspective, you will have insightful ideas and make important personal discoveries. A practice such as mindfulness meditation teaches you to slow down your racing thoughts, release negativity, and calm both your mind and body. "Techniques can vary, but in general, mindfulness meditation involves deep breathing and awareness of body and mind. Practicing mindfulness meditation doesn't require props or preparation (no need for candles, essential oils, or mantras, unless you enjoy them). To get started, all you need is a comfortable place to sit, three to five minutes of free time, and a judgment-free mindset." Regular practice of mindfulness meditation has benefits for your physical as well as your mental health, including reduced stress, lower heart rate, improved immunity, and better sleep (Cherry 2022).

4. When you have a spark, practice being a skeptical optimist. By this I mean, question and test your ideas so you know they can stand up in reality. The functionality is that the idea needs to actually work or possess some degree of usefulness. Skeptics are critical thinkers. They look beyond the surface and dig deeper. Skepticism is good because it keeps your mind open, but never fall

prey to cynicism because that closes your mind again. To be successful, you need a default setting of optimism.

5. Have associative thinking. Associative thinking is fast, subconscious thinking that associates one concept with another. The ideas can involve memories, emotions, and physical sensations. Associative thinking is the ability to connect previously unconnected ideas. Leveraging this skill, people can generate different options quickly. Innovators with this skill can see things in new ways and imagine disruptive new business models, products, and services. Jeff Dyer, coauthor of *The Innovator's DNA*, shared that you have to act differently to think differently (Dyer, Gregersen, and Christensen 2011).

6. Embrace divergent thinking. Divergent thinking, also known as lateral thinking, is the process of creating multiple unique ideas or solutions to a problem you are trying to solve. Business leaders can foster this skill while increasing morale and encouraging flexibility by not dismissing the first idea and instead encouraging their teams to think outside the box and exercise their creativity. This is important in the brainstorming process (Airfocus 2022).

7. Don't criticize ideas. None of the ideas you generate should be treated with "yes, but…" or "no, because…" This kills creativity. Don't "kill" ideas prematurely. Instead, allow the good ideas to float to the surface among the lesser ones. Just let them naturally fade away once you focus on one or two great ideas. Also, avoid naysayers at early stages of brainstorming and idea-generation or prototyping. Find a balance for your criticism as it is useful, just not the type that is fearful of risk or unknowns.

8. Be nimble and flexible in your thinking so you don't see failure as a bad thing. It's not a bad thing at all. Failure pushes a willingness to change our mind, experiment, test, and work to improve. In my opinion, failure is an opportunity for growth.

9. View other people's ideas and creativity as a springboard to inspire ideas you can build on by using them to spark your own slant or modifications and build upon ideas and creativity of others. This doesn't mean your idea is lacking in originality.

10. Don't collect and hide your ideas out of fear. Instead, share them to learn other people's suggestions and tips for improvement, such as in a collaborative environment.

11. Know when to rest an idea so it moves from the focus of your brain to the passive mind like it's in marinating mode, which often helps you come up with a better solution, such as after a good night's rest when you were not actively looking for solutions.

Maya Angelou also suggested that thinking creativity helps foster even greater creativity (Posture 2020):

"Creativity or talent, like electricity, is something I don't understand but something I'm able to harness and use. While electricity remains a mystery, I know I can plug into it and light up a cathedral, a synagogue, or an operating room and use it to help save a life. Or I can use it to electrocute someone. Like electricity, creativity makes no judgment. I can use it productively or destructively. The important thing is to use it. You can't use up creativity. The more you use it, the more you have."

KEY
TAKEAWAYS
Chapter 6

- A creative mindset is really about opening up new ways of thinking to allow you to express your creativity, recognizing inspiration, and viewing the world with a little more wonder and awe.

- Our mindset plays a significant role in determining our achievement and success.

- Be curious. When you have a desire to learn more about a variety of things, you'll be able to draw upon a wide variety of knowledge and insights. This increases the chances that you'll make connections that spark ideas.

- High IQ doesn't mean high degree of creativity. If you want to boost your creativity, then looking at things in a fresh, almost playful way, mixed with curiosity, discipline and a passion to explore and know more will bring you on the creative path.

- Adopt a gratitude or mindfulness practice. When you build in time for a spiritual practice, you are surrendering to opening yourself up to receiving.

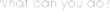
What can you do?

Create a Gratitude Journal!

Try to shift your focus from what you want, to what you have. This helps you appreciate the everyday happenings in the present moment. This conscious appreciation of your life experience can increase one's happiness. as well as reduce stress and inflammation. This in turn can positively impact your health and wellness.

Make an effort daily to record 1-3 people or experiences that you are grateful for. If you're not into writing, try using your calendar to write 1 grateful something and why. Still not comfortable? Try sharing your gratitude item daily as dinner with family. Ask that everyone share what they are grateful for too. Explain why and be specific.

We all have goals we want to achieve. Did you know you're more likely to achieve your goal if you commit to it in writing? This happens because, when you write, it increases your chance of remembering (Murphy 2018).

Creating an action plan is the key to making your goals attainable. You can't create an action plan if you don't have a clear description of your desired outcome. Write down a goal with specific objectives, such as using the SMART framework coined by George Doran in the November 1981 issue of the Management Review. The acronym stands for: Specific, measurable, attainable, relevant, and time-bound (Boitnott 2019).

Each element of the SMART framework works together to create a goal that is carefully planned, clear, and trackable. Now, using this approach, here's a quick breakdown of what each letter represents so you can get started on creating your goals (Herrity 2022)!

Specific: Be as clear and specific as possible with what you want to achieve. At this step, you should answer your six "W" questions: who, what, where, when, which, and why.

Measurable: What evidence will prove you're mak-ing progress toward your goal? Identify precise times, amounts, or other units that measure your progress toward a goal. Setting milestones along the way with small but meaningful rewards as you progress is effec-tive too.

Attainable: Stretch the limits of what you think is pos-sible. While they're not impossible to complete, they're often challenging and full of obstacles; hence why the plan will help you to get there!

Relevant: Each of your goals should align with your values and larger, long-term goals and focus on what you truly desire. They are in harmony with everything that is important in your life, from success in your career to happiness with the people you love.

Time-bound: What is the goal timeframe? An end date can help provide motivation and help you prioritize. Time-bound goals are challenging and grounding.

Now you have all the tools to use this space to craft your own SMART goals. Go for it!

Additional Space to Reflect

Get going on those SMART goals here!

CHAPTER 7

CREATIVE HEALING

Creativity helps us perceive the world in new and different ways. I run a monthly creativity club for a group of women online. Several of the women have never even painted or done anything creative. This group was formed to try something new and to allow time for a creative, mindful practice. The women who aren't normally creative decided to join because they were after the mindful benefits, despite their skepticism around the creative part.

Each month, I choose a topic that introduces a new medium and teaches a subject that's easy enough for beginners not to feel self-conscious, yet flexible enough for a more advanced participant to spread their wings and display their skills. Prior to each session, I send out a materials list so participants can buy what they need to join in while building up their creative inventory. The feedback has been overwhelmingly positive. The self-proclaimed "non-creatives" are loyal and come to every session. One woman said she now feels like she's more creative in her work and sees the world much differently, with a deeper appreciation for what's around her. Another woman shared that the time we spend together feels so good to her soul because she's made new acquaintances while having deep, focused time to concentrate on something new and using a different part of her mind than she does in her daily life. It's typically in the evening, so I try to make it fun and playful.

Whether it's creating something of beauty or solving a problem, there's a sense of recharge and refreshment that engaging in a creative endeavor has on our bodies and minds. It's basically a prescription for your mental health. In their book *Creative Healing: How to Heal Yourself by Tapping Your Hidden Creativity*, authors Michael Samuels and Mary Rockwood Lane address the impact of creativity on freeing your inner healer by finding the artist within you. They propose that prayer, art, and healing come from the human soul and, therefore, creativity is honoring the self. When creative arts are used for their own healing power, rather than their interpretation or therapy, it brings a sense of accomplishment, peace, and well-being and makes us feel good (Samuels and Lane 2011).

In hospitals, for example, art is used, along with gardens, to create a positive distraction for patients, which reduces their discomfort and anxiety. When you enter a hospital, notice the music at the entrance and how its soft sound that evokes relation prepares the visitor for an openness to healing. Art at the patient's bedside promotes a more comfortable and creative environment. The process itself of creating art is healing, so setting up a space in your home for it, near nature with sunlight, will connect you to the outside—the sounds and sights—and inspire a special art space.

According to their website, "The National Organization for Arts in Health, NOAH provides transformational leadership to bring the field of arts in health together and to move the field forward. Our focus is on the future of arts, health, and wellbeing, and creating tangible impact from our goals and initiatives. We know through research and experience that the arts are an integral component to health, and we are committed to shaping a reality where that fact is accepted fully and incorporated into medical treatment, medical education, prevention, and public health and wellbeing" (National Organization for Arts in Health 2022).

Art therapy has been around since the 1940s. Two pioneers in the field, Margaret Naumburg and Edith Kramer, used art therapy to help clients tap into their inner thoughts, feelings, and experiences through creative expression. Therapists use patients' free-form art expressions to encourage them to talk about the images and begin to look to themselves for meaning and insight (Art Therapy 2022).

In her book, *The Art Therapy Sourcebook*, Cathy Malchiodi, a leading expert in today's art therapy movement, states that, through art therapy, "people may find relief from overwhelming emotions, crises, or trauma. They may discover insights about themselves, increase their sense of well-being, enrich their daily lives through creative expression, or experience personal transformation" (Malchiodi 2006).

There's a healing power to creativity. It's been proven to reduce pain, stress, and anxiety, which is why it's so beneficial for people with mental distress, especially mood disorders. This is why art therapy has become increasingly popular for trauma victims or those coping with shame, depression, or anger. There's a relief that comes from art, whether it's visual, musical, or performance.

There are physical benefits as well. Art increases immunity, balances hormones, and influences the autonomic nervous system to increase relaxation.

One reason might be the concept of flow, which is what the participant of my monthly group was referring to when she said she can focus and concentrate in a way she hasn't experienced before. Psychologist Mihaly Csikszentmihalyi's popular 1990 book, *Flow: The Psychology of Optimal Experience*, is based on the premise that happiness levels can be shifted by introducing flow. He refers to this as a "flow state." It's also referred to as "being in the zone." Flow is associated with subjective well-being, satisfaction with life, and general happiness. At work, it's linked to productivity, motivation, and company loyalty (Robb 2019). Csikszentmihalyi developed the term "flow state" because many of the people he interviewed described their optimal states of performance as instances when their work simply flowed out of them without much effort (Csikszentmihalyi 2008).

Csikszentmihalyi's studies led him to conclude that happiness is an internal state of being, not an external one. Happiness is not a rigid, unchanging state, Csikszentmihalyi has argued. On the contrary, the manifestation of happiness takes a committed effort.

Beyond each person's set point of happiness, there is a level of happiness over which each individual has some degree of control. Through research, Csikszentmihalyi began to understand that people are their most creative, productive, and happy when they are in a state of flow.

In Csikszentmihalyi's words, flow is "a state in which people are so involved in an activity that nothing else seems to matter; the experience is so enjoyable that people will continue to do it even at great cost, for the sheer sake of doing it" (Oppland 2016).

It's important to note that one can't experience flow if distractions disrupt the experience (Nakamura et al., 2009). In order to experience this state, one would need to turn off their smartphone. "Inducing flow is about the balance between the level of skill and the size of the challenge at hand" (Miller 2019). It is an important component of creativity and well-being, as well as self-actualization.

The freedom to play and explore is powerful. As adults, engaging in a playful, non-judgmental place, void of expectations and criticisms or pressures, inspires a sense of recharge and refresh. This impacts a person's health and well-being. "Playing is just as important for adults as it is for children. Among its many benefits, adult play can boost your creativity, sharpen your sense of humor, and help you cope better with stress" (Marais 2022).

In a 2011 study, playfulness in adults was linked to characteristics such as liking to make people laugh, the ability to ease tension, and being able to support creative processes in a group. They found that higher playfulness scores were associated with higher creativity, appreciating beauty, approaching life with excitement and energy, playful expressions of love, a sense of hope, and a sense of humor (Proyer and Ruch 2011).

In a 2013 study, researchers found that playful adults reported having lower stress levels. Play also helped them use healthier coping styles, like acceptance and positive reframing (Prayer 2013).

Dr. Stuart Brown, researcher and founder of The National Institute for Play, defines the play state in his book, *Play: How It Shapes the Brain, Opens the Imagination, and Invigorates the*

Soul, as a "state of mind that one has when absorbed in an activity that provides enjoyment and a suspension of sense of time." In his book, he identified eight "play personalities" that can help identify what specific types of play work best for different people (Brown and Vaughan 2009).

The benefits of play include:

- Relieving stress.

- Preventing memory problems and improve brain function.

- Stimulating the mind and imagination, boosting creativity, and helping you adapt and solve problems.

- Improving relationships and connection to others.

- Feeling young and energetic (Robinson et al. 2022).

Ironically, when discussing creativity, most people comment with the standard "I'm not creative." What they don't understand is that they may not identify as artistic, but deep down, everyone is creative. They are getting caught up in the end product, having an inner critic, and fearing judgment, and that's not what creativity is really about.

According to the science, we make new neuropathways and increase connectivity in the brain, enhance well-being, and improve motivation when we engage in creative endeavors.

The National Institute for Play underscores the research that already exists on play. "A huge amount of existing scientific research—from neurophysiology, developmental and cognitive psychology, to animal play behavior, and evolutionary and molecular biology—contains rich data on play. The existing research describes patterns and states of play and explains how play shapes our brains, creates our competencies, and ballasts our emotions" (National Institute of Play 2014).

A study titled "Creativity in the Wild: Improving Creative Reasoning through Immersion in Natural Settings" showed how nature affects creativity. A group of hikers who spent four days immersed in nature and disconnected from technological devices increased performance on a creativity/problem-solving task by 50 percent (Landers 2022).

Nature in this study provided emotionally positive stimuli. By reducing the usage of phones and computers, those in the study weren't switching tasks or multi-tasking, attending to sudden events, maintaining task goals, or inhibiting irrelevant actions. Therefore, spending quality time in nature improved their creativity test scores.

Creativity is the brain's food. The following are health benefits associated with creativity:

- Increases happiness

- Elevates mood

- Alleviates anxiety

- Reduces dementia

- Improves mental health

- Boosts immune system (prevents disease)

- Boosts brain function and increases intelligence

Creativity is a wellness practice. It doesn't matter what medium you choose to express yourself, only that you choose to. By engaging in a creative activity, you're giving yourself a gift of well-being.

Some benefits on your life from a creativity practice include:

- Deeper engagement in work or career

- Increased excitement and enthusiasm

- Uncovering more inspiration in daily life

- Developing the mindset of a deep thinker and finding deeper meaning

- Improving personal connections and enjoyment in life

Next time you have a creative block or get stuck on a problem, move away from the computer. It helps to think creatively about solutions and alternative options while walking in the garden or even doodling on a blank sheet of paper.

KEY
TAKEAWAYS
Chapter 7

- Whether it's creating something of beauty or solving a problem, there's a sense of recharge and refreshment that engaging in a creative endeavor has on our bodies and minds. It's basically a prescription for your mental health.

- There's a healing power to creativity. It's been proven to reduce pain, stress, and anxiety, which is why it's so beneficial for people with mental distress, especially mood disorders. This is why art therapy has become increasingly popular for trauma victims or those coping with shame, depression, or anger. There's a relief that comes from art, whether it's visual, musical, or performance.

- When you capture a moment of "flow", you tap into deeper focus and concentration. This is an optimal state of performance is associated with satisfaction with life happiness.

- The freedom to play and explore is powerful. As adults, engaging in a playful, non-judgmental place, void of expectations and criticisms or pressures, inspires a sense of recharge and refresh.

- Ignore your inner critic. Everyone has the gift of creativity.

What can you do?

Pick up a coloring book and a box of crayons or colored pencils.

Keep it on your desk to use when you're feeling stressed. It's amazing how coloring can calm you down.

Working on a big project and can't come up with ideas? Take a 5-10 minute break that includes your coloring book and crayons. You'll be amazed how it will spark ideas, get you out of stagnation and into flow.

Doodling is, in my opinion, an underrated art form. It's an opportunity to experiment and play while practic-ing your drawing skills. Doodling, for me, is free flow, usually random shapes connected with dots and blocks. Mostly nonsensible scribbles, it provides a focus and clarity similar to what I feel from meditating. Check out these doodle artists for some inspiration:

- Joe Whale, a.k.a. Doodle Boy
- Mr. Doodle
- Visoth Kakvei
- Hattie Stewert
- Eva-Lotta Lamm
- Matt Lyon
- Fred Blunt
- Lizzie Mary Cullen
- Pat Perry
- Kerby Rosanes
- Lisa Krasse
- Jim Bradshaw
- Chris Piascik
- Sagaki Keita
- Chris Glasz

Now grab a pen or a pencil and get doodling on the next page!

Space to Draw

Use this space to complete the reflection for this chapter.

CHAPTER 8

GOING AGAINST THE GRAIN

Ideas come from unexpected places. I may be putting on my clothes, or be in the shower, and, all of a sudden, something comes to me. Then, later in the day, I might realize it wasn't a great idea after all. Sometimes a meeting with an outside team could provide a different way of looking at something that might lead to an insight too.

For many people who have suffered injustices, trust is a key challenge they struggle to overcome. Even for people without such negative experiences, trust is a frequent issue to contend with. It is a basic principle we must deal with in all relationships and interactions. That's why, in the workplace, trust is a key issue for employees to help create a sense of unity to overcome obstacles, celebrate wins, and represent the brand. In addition to the trust you show to your team, you must also enable confidence to flow between employees, teams, and departments. A culture of fear hinders innovation and growth.

According to Dr. Robert (a.k.a. Bob) Giancalone, creativity has both helped and hindered his academic career. He shared that early on in the process, creativity allowed him the freedom to have fun and explore, and it empowered him in a positive way.

Bob speaks about creativity as his ability to identify problems and find solutions. He's also quick to add that he doesn't have an artistic bone in his body, but he does have an intuition that enabled him to see and synthesize things other people had not yet seen. He flatly attributes his financial success to his creativity, but candidly admits that many people really don't understand the creative mind or view creativity as a positive trait. His desire to be true to who he is, to not play the game, and to go to the beat of his own drum was often professionally isolating as he lost allies who didn't see the potential of his ideas.

"To follow the road where it goes as opposed to as it is planned is not linear and often perceived as weird."

This non-conformist, rebellious slant came from accepting early on in his career that acceptance from people doesn't matter to him. "I am who I am. That's the only way I know to be." And so he was able to overcome adversity and use what might be perceived as a negative to create an opportunity. In turn, he tends to gravitate toward the like-minded—people willing to put themselves out there and go against the grain. For Bob, he is not able to replicate, as what he does to illicit a creative solution one time may not help the next, yet he finds the creativity to come from more of a flow state. He lives life with his antenna up, seeking connections and opportunities to propel the next idea then working to interpret which ideas are worth moving forward on and taking a risk for. Not all ideas are worth the risk, but the ones that are made the challenges worthwhile in the end.

However, while I realize Bob's ability to disengage from the social pressures and expectations often imposed in the workplace is admirable, it's not realistic for everyone. To that end, I wanted to learn about the impact that constraints have on a person's creativity. I had the opportunity to interview an employee of a large financial institution. The way he explained it to me is his role is like an "academic position," in the sense that it's "publish or perish." He requested anonymity, as he wanted to be open with his experience since it offers a valuable perspective.

The role requires a continuous churning out of research that is accepted into high-level peer reviewed journals, or as he explained, "It's definitely a kiss of death if you stop researching. Then they'll just move you out. While there's an invitation to be creative, to come up with something new, there's going to be certain directions that are strongly discouraged." While this is likely nothing new in science in particular, you can write something that you think is fantastic only to find a lot of resistance from people who have vested interests in the old ways or just don't want to be confronted with a different way of thinking. This feels like an uphill battle and has had an impact on this researcher where he had a very tough time getting some work published.

"I think part of it is just, people are reluctant to look at the thing from a different perspective. It's asking them to learn a little bit something new. And, you know, it's just easier to say no, you know. The famous people aren't talking about this. So I'm not really interested."

When asked about the effect on his morale, he explained that it can be difficult when working on something where you think you've made a big contribution only to find it's been rejected.

In his work, it's two-fold. His colleagues may support an idea, but it could go to a journal and get rejected, or worse, he's not even given a chance to defend it, which feels like it's not even receiving a fair shot.

Regarding the culture and whether he feels like he has allies, sadly, he has not found his colleagues nor boss to be as supportive as he had hoped. In fact, his boss sometimes appears dismissive of the topics he finds important or encourages him to chase the latest fad, which he finds especially annoying, given that he prefers to do something more novel and can allow him to stand out a bit above the crowd. "It's hard to stay motivated to keep pushing on when your boss thinks it's not worth you spending time on." Despite the challenges, he feels a rebellious mindset would be difficult, but trying to look at things differently is helpful.

When I asked him what prevents him from pursing his real interests, he explained that perhaps some of it is probably fear and part of it might be hope that eventually it'll rise to the top, but in the meantime, he works to come up with different ways in other papers to sell it or to keep pushing it with his colleagues. At the same time, "I have to be willing to just let it go and say, 'Okay, that's in the hands of God,' you know. It's okay. And he's really in charge of my career at the end of the day. So I just keep doing the best I can try to work under him and let him decide.

"The rebel's superpower is challenge. Everything can be reexamined. There is no reason to stay with tradition or norm. Immense strength comes from taking a different position and challenging what everybody else views as normal. This gives the rebel the benefit of perspective, and they see things in a way that no one else does."

I remember once when I was working on a big project for a large, traditional company and proposed an alternative solution to a challenge we were faced with. The leadership thought I was mad, and they didn't hide their skepticism. I stood by my suggestion, and while it was uncomfortable to deal with the negativity purely due to their lack of understanding, I used the opportunity to educate the team and gain their support. As with Bob, his rebelliousness enabled him to be productive in his work as the ideas kept flowing to him, even despite not always being accepted. Don't be afraid—embrace it!

KEY
TAKEAWAYS
Chapter 8

- A culture of fear hinders innovation and growth.

- Trusting your intuition will enable you to see and synthesize things other people might not see.

- Try not to hold back or let expectations and standards get in the way of presenting your ideas.

- Gain the trust of the people around you by standing true to your values, and mixing confidence with compassion.

- Understand your environment, observe and inquire, so you comprehend the pulse and culture well-enough to anticipate how to proceed and what the results might be.

- When presenting an alternative idea, use the opportunity to educate the team and gain their support.

- Don't be afraid—embrace it!

What can you do?

If you're someone that tends to hold themselves back from contributing in ways that go against the grain, ask yourself why. What are you afraid of or concerned about?

If you're bold and willing to put yourself and your ideas out there, why?

What risks are you willing to take to stand up for something you believe in?

According to Harvard behavioral scientist Francesca Gino, being a rebel and breaking the rules makes you a better leader. One thing you can do to lead like a rebel is find freedom in constraints. Constraints provide focus by limiting your options. They define a safe space where you can exercise your creativity and help you explore what's possible given the limitations (Schwantes 2018). Look around the room and identify an object such as a lamp or a chair. Now, in the space below, draw that object without lifting your pencil from the paper. You can also try this by drawing with your eyes closed or with your non-dominant hand as a constraint. Have fun!

CREATIVE DISCERNMENT

In the dead of night, when the house was dark and quiet, I would often find myself tucked away in a makeshift studio in my parents' basement. I was around twenty years old and bursting with ideas, curiosities, and a deep desire to create. While I could feel the creative process was deeply spiritual, I wouldn't have thought of creativity as a spiritual function. Yet, according to Ignatian spirituality, "Creativity is woven into all creation [...] I encounter the sacred while in the act of creating. Thus, creativity fits into the First Principle and Foundation; it is a gift of this life that God intends for the good of my soul and of others' souls" (Wright 2019).

The psychology of creativity knows much more about how people generate ideas than about how they judge their own ideas. The first question to ask is, how accurate are people's judgments of their ideas? When you look at how people self-report on all sorts of matters, it's clear this accuracy varies. According to research, originality and accuracy are correlated; therefore, people with more creative ideas also judge them more accurately. Further, the judgment and concept of fluency were also factors in a person's degree of accuracy. So, what does this mean about creativity? People higher in discernment had traits that characterize creative people. Creative people, thereby, can come up with good ideas and discern which ideas are the good ones (Silvia 2008).

When you're feeling the nudge, the gentle pull from an uncertain place, you're sensing that subtly from your heightened awareness, acceptance, and willingness to see beyond. You're paying attention to what's around you, attending to the details that feed the spark of creativity. When you're immersed in a creative task, it's very similar to meditating or praying. You have a willingness to "be" and let unknown forces guide your final outcome. Trust is an opportunity to reflect, a willingness to be vulnerable, and an ability to discern.

According to Dictionary.com, discernment is the ability to obtain sharp perceptions or to judge well (Dictionary.com 2022). In the creative realm, you reflect and see things from various angles, sparking curiosity, asking questions, seeking answers within from experience, yet looking deeper and bigger. We learn from our creative endeavors as much as we teach. When you use discernment with creativity, you are distinguishing right from wrong, from necessary and relevant to unnecessary and indifferent. Discernment is more than a process; it's about having a critical eye enough to objectively critique your idea to see where it fits in to good, better, or best to decide if it's worth the risk to take the next step. It's worth putting yourself out on a limb, to face your fears, knowing in the end you'll move forward with an insight or creation you believe is worth the risk.

Discernment isn't the light bulb or sudden spark of an idea. It's the inner pull toward something that insists you pay attention.

Once you have discerned and decided that you will pay attention, the next step of creativity requires a hearty dose of healthy detachment. Once you decide your idea is worth the emotional investment—of "putting yourself out there"—you agree to an unwritten contract that requires you have trust in the process and won't try to control it. You must be patient and follow the journey where the road may take you. This is where, if you believe in a higher power, you trust in God or source for where the final destination will take you. You might be generating ideas left and right, but your willingness to pursue an idea after thoughtful evaluation suggests an openness to experience something further.

"I soon came to realize that 'putting yourself out there' is just a nice way of reminding you to *not* get caught in your comfort zone. Life is much too short to constantly prioritize staying in that comfort zone over your own personal growth."

Think about it a little like dating or meeting new people, just with ideas—there's a need for a willingness to be vulnerable. Dr. Martha Tara Lee, a clinical sexologist (DHS, MA, BA), dating expert, and founder of Eros Coaching, says, "It's easy to get caught up in the same thoughts, beliefs, and attitudes by doing and being the same-old. But it's important to realize that breaking up these periods of autopilot by stepping out of your comfort zone is all part of what it means to open up to life's possibilities."

BE CONFIDENT WITH YOUR CREATIVITY

Discernment, this ability to essentially evaluate the creativity or value of your own idea, is an important component of psychological theories of creativity. It requires truth-seeking, wisdom, and an ability to ask and answer difficult questions. It's not about confirming something you know or hope. It requires a willingness to be wrong as much as being right and a self-reflective yet investigative mindset to seek and find your directional pull on the matter. When you use discernment, you reflect on the issue. Take, for example, this chapter—perhaps my claim is this chapter is complete. So I would reflect on the words on this page and think about the reality of what I know, then compare with what I have and ask myself what I need to add or eliminate to make this feel complete. I would weigh one with the other and use inner wisdom as a guide to tell me the truth, not what I want to hear. This requires patience to take the time to be thorough in your understanding and in the alternatives. Using discernment trains you to pay attention and reflect. It teaches that some things are bigger than they appear and instills a healthy dose of attachment to what was created. When you use discernment, you can rest easier with your decisions.

KEY
TAKEAWAYS
Chapter 9

- When you're immersed in a creative task, it's very similar to meditating or praying. You have a willingness to "be" and let unknown forces guide your final outcome. Trust is an opportunity to reflect, a willingness to be vulnerable, and an ability to discern.

- Discernment isn't the light bulb or sudden spark of an idea. It's the inner pull toward something that insists you pay attention.

- Discernment, this ability to essentially evaluate the creativity or value of your own idea, is an important component of psychological theories of creativity. It requires truth-seeking, wisdom, and an ability to ask and answer difficult questions.

- You must be patient and follow the journey where the road may take you. This is where, if you believe in a higher power, you trust in God or source for where the final destination will take you.

- Using discernment trains you to pay attention and reflect.

What can you do?

Discernment requires truth-seeking.

Some ideas or creative solutions might seem fabulous, but upon further reflection, appear less than ideal. The willingness to let go of an idea or modify can be challenging.

Asking yourself why what you've created has value and warrants staying. Look at your concept honestly. To evaluate, think about what you've created, what the reality is and comapre the two.

Reflect within and listen.

Discernment and decision-making is an essential life skill. I believe some of the basic elements of discernment can help us make important decisions. Take a moment to think about an issue in your life that requires a decision. Use the space to write down a sentence describing the issue. Below the statement, you'll create two columns. Label the column on the left "Pros" and the one on the right "Cons." Now, under each column, dump everything on your mind under the appropriate label. Then take a few moments to feel and think about what each of the pros and cons means to you and to the outcome of the decision you need to make. Next, write a reflection on what this activity revealed to you.

Pros	Cons

More Space to Reflect

Use this space to compete the reflection for this chapter.

CHAPTER 10
SELF-TRUST

Ralph Waldo Emerson is quoted as saying, "Self-trust is the first secret to success" (O'Toole 2019). Trust is not static; it is dynamic. When you take small steps toward trusting yourself and listening to your inner voice, you eliminate your self-doubt and see opportunity instead of limitation.

One aspect of the process of creativity is the perception of your value or self-esteem and how deserving you see yourself of success. This is combined with one's belief they are likely to succeed and believe in their ability. Self-confidence is something someone exudes. It comes from within.

"Self-trust is a necessary condition of personal autonomy and self-respect. Self-trust involves a positive sense of the motivations and competence of the trusted person; a willingness to depend on him or her; and an acceptance of vulnerability" (Govier 1993).

It seems, then, self-trust is a learned skill that requires both emotional and analytical skills, but since choice is involved, the person must rely on their own inner navigation or resources. It can be the inner critic or your biggest cheerleader. "Self-trust is not trusting yourself to know all the answers, nor is it believing that you will always do the right things. It's having the conviction that you will be kind and respectful to yourself regardless of the outcome of your efforts" (Bloom and Bloom 2019).

Defined as "self-reliance" and "faith in oneself," Cynthia Wall, author of *The Courage to Trust*, explains it is both a learnable skill, emotion and a choice to be made in each moment (Wall 2005).

People who are self-trusting tend to have clarity and confidence in their decisions. Self-trusting people are not overly dependent nor independent people who access their wisdom or authority from a deep place within while not coming off as arrogant. People who trust in themselves are able to learn from their experiences (both the successes and failures) and are keen and mindful observers. They have an ability to look at an experience without fear of self-punishment, which means they are not worried about protecting themselves from external or internal disapproval and, therefore, are more open to accessing teaching moments from their experiences (Bloom and Bloom 2019).

So, what happens when you have not honed your self-trust skill?

On a recent *Unmistakable Creative* podcast episode, Daniel Pink spoke about his new book called *The Power of Regret*. He explains that regret can be an incredibly powerful emotion—both capable of holding us back, but also of propelling us forward. His extensive research illustrated why we should embrace our regrets and use them as a force for good. In his own research, he collected, sorted, and catalogued through thousands of self-reported regrets. What he found was the collection of memories still cause pain for people even decades after the events occurred. He concluded there are what he considers the four kinds of regrets: foundational (things we could have done earlier in life that would have made our lives better); boldness (being hesitant and unwilling to take risks); moral (violating standards we know are correct); and connection (failing to engage with others). Some are light and fleeting while others are heartbreaking (Pink 2022).

Brené Brown, a research professor at the University of Houston, has spent her career studying courage, vulnerability, empathy, and shame. She posted the following on Facebook about how the emotion of regret can be used for a higher purpose:

"I've found regret to be one of the most powerful emotional reminders that change and growth are necessary. In fact, I've come to believe that regret is a kind of package deal: A function of empathy, it's a call to courage and a path toward wisdom.

Like all emotions, regret can be used constructively or destructively, but the wholesale dismissal of regret is wrongheaded and dangerous. 'No regrets' doesn't mean living with courage, it means living without reflection.

To live without regret is to believe you have nothing to learn, no amends to make, and no opportunity to be braver with your life. I'm not suggesting that we have to live with regret, but I do think it's important to allow ourselves to experience and feel it" (ForCreativeGirls 2018).

Igniting us to take action, signaling what we see as an opportunity in life, and helping us embrace imperfection, TEDx speaker Kathryn Schulz, who in her talk "Don't regret regrets," speaks in praise of the universal emotion. "We need to learn to love the flawed, imperfect things that we create and to forgive ourselves for creating them," she says.

"The bigger the regret, the deeper the shame, and the bigger the opportunity. Just like being compassionate and forgiving for another person who may have harmed us, we can focus that same attitude toward ourselves. When we demonstrate that we have learned from the mistake, regret evaporates. Then self-forgiveness and self-trust automatically occur. We are producing evidence that reflects the integration of what we have learned" (Bloom and Bloom 2019).

"People who have not learned to relate to their inner critical voice in a productive way will argue with it or comply with its indictments. When we buy into the negative voice, we diminish our self-trust. Trying to escape the inner critic and ignoring it by drinking or drugging, or other distractions, will empower it. The way to build self-trust is to relate to the inner critic and show it that it is taking a seed of truth and blowing it out of proportion" (Bloom and Bloom 2019).

How can parents, for example, foster an environment that helps to ensure our children grow up with an ability to rely on their own self-trust skills? What conditions foster this growth? How can parents encourage their children to trust themselves? It seems to me that self-trust builds confidence, which, in turn, produces a willingness to trust the process and be vulnerable if you're putting yourself "out there," as one might when sharing an idea or creation.

When you find yourself in unfamiliar territory, often people will retreat to familiarity as an excuse when, actually, it's fear of judgment that stifles their confidence and sabotages the outcome. Often, when asked to perform a creative task or apply creative problem-solving to find a solution, people will opt-out and exclaim they aren't creative. David Kelley of IDEO explains this as their fear of judgment making them uncomfortable. In his experience, when working with groups of people who have declared themselves as "not creative," once the person learned the process, gave it a try, and had small successes, they gained confidence. This confidence, in turn, moved them from fear to familiarity and was often transformational in helping them realize they do, in fact, have natural creativity.

Being raised in an environment where someone feels free from judgment or criticism provides a space conducive to cultivating a child's budding self-trust. Unconditional positive regard (UPR) was developed by Stanley Standal in 1954 and popularized by Carl Rogers, father of humanistic psychology. When we are aware of our unique strengths, we have a heightened sense of trust for that which we know we excel at and are more likely to engage and share said talents with others (Cherry 2020).

If you feel you are lacking self-trust in certain areas, consider viewing trust as something you must earn from yourself. Perhaps there are some areas where you already feel confident and trust your ability, while other areas you might need to work on earning more trust from yourself in order to move forward and gain confidence. Make a list of these areas and what might be helpful to do to increase your self-trust. This is an opportunity for growth, not a flaw in character.

Another way to teach or learn self-trust is by encouraging opportunities to excavate deep and look for answers. Parents might ask their children questions to encourage conversations that generate how a child might feel or what they feel to help establish that much valued self-reliance with which trust is associated. For adults, asking yourself how you feel about various situations is certainly important, but consciously diving deep through journaling, meditation, or even doodling can have tremendous value in working to answer the big questions that foster self-trust.

As we recognize ourselves as skillful in a given area, the ability to extend self-trust is developed. This can't be one-off excavation. The benefits come from habit and reinforcement.

Carol Dweck referred to this as the "power of yet." She explained that she once learned of a school that gave students the grade "not yet." Similarly, this inspired students to explore and continue verses finish and end. So often we find ourselves in unfamiliar territory, but our willingness to explore and listen for the gentle pull toward our inner passion, desire, or voice of inspiration is hindered by our perceptions of what success is or what is expected of us (Dweck 2014).

If we find ourselves limited by our organizational culture and blinded by our fear of judgment or criticism, we allow ourselves to surrender to the unknown. When we are children, we look for alternative ways to get what we want to find a solution. Then, at some point, we see definition and barriers to our imagination. When we stop seeking alternatives, we push our creativity aside in favor of logic. As a child, we allow our inner guide to direct us toward answers. As adults, we quiet that inquiry for practicality.

The cause and effect of when we raise the bar on our personal expectations, thinking, for example, that we need to create the best solution or masterpiece before we share it, is a sure creativity blocker. Hinging results on an unrealistic outcome is doomed to be uncreative. Besides, when we allow ourselves to fail, we open the door to reveal what we are good at and what we are likely to succeed at. Failure also illuminates what we assigned value to enough to pursue, sends a reminder of our purpose and provides an opportunity for gratitude in the simple things, and removes the waste from our lives that limits our access to creativity. When we remove the limitations, we acknowledge a willingness to enter a sort of construction zone for our lives where we are a work in progress.

"Creativity comes from trust," explained author Rita Mae Brown. Creative expression emerges when we trust our instincts and allow ourselves permission to act on the gentle pull to create. Self-trust appears to be the precursor to creativity and intuition. Self-trust enables us to tap into a sort of comfort that promotes trusting our intuition, which, in turn, pushes us to trust our creativity (internetPoem 2022).

The bottom line is that, as the architects of our lives, we own the right to feed what brings us joy and pleasure, and feeding the creativity is a gift we can use to help us on that journey.

Alan Alda explained creativity as going into the "place where no one else has ever been" (Goodreads 2008).

"Being caught in the past or worrying about the future undermines self-trust." If we are fearful of or always worrying about what might be, then we are missing out on opportunities to actually "be" what we desire. Be courageous and take action, so you can live in the present, so we can learn and grow free from fear and open to possibility (Goodreads 2008).

In his book *Creative Pep Talk*, Andy Miller gathers advice and insights from fifty of today's leading creative professionals (Miller 2017). Some of the advice that stood out were the simple reminders of gratitude, appreciate what is born out of talent, everyone has a story to tell, it's important to learn to say no and respect yourself and your talent, embrace mistakes, take risks, be brave and strong, learn from adversity, and that there's a value in fostering focused play.

KEY TAKEAWAYS
Chapter 10

- One aspect of the process of creativity is the perception of your value or self-esteem and how deserving you see yourself of success. This is combined with one's belief they are likely to succeed and believe in their ability. Self-confidence is something someone exudes. It comes from within.

- People who are self-trusting tend to have clarity and confidence in their decisions. Self-trusting people are not overly dependent nor independent people who access their wisdom or authority from a deep place within

- People who trust in themselves are able to learn from their experiences (both the successes and failures) and are keen and mindful observers.

- Regret can be an incredibly powerful emotion— both capable of holding us back, but also of propelling us forward.

- When we buy into the negative voice, we diminish our self-trust.

What can you do?

If you feel you are lacking self-trust in certain areas, consider viewing trust as something you must earn from yourself.

Think of some areas where you already feel confident and trust your ability, as well as other areas you might need to work on earning more trust from yourself in order to move forward and gain confidence.

Make a list of these areas and what might be helpful to do to increase your self-trust. This is an opportunity for growth, this is not a flaw in character.

You are awesome! I mean it. You are—believe it!

Write down three things about yourself that make you the unique and amazing human you are. Not just one-word answers here... write a sentence for each. Explain why and how this nugget of awesomeness you've identified makes you extraordinary.

CHAPTER 11

BE A CREATIVE REBEL

I grew up before hair gel was a thing. My long dark hair was frizzy, crazy, and wild. Moms would often comment on how much they wished they had my curls, while, to many kids, my hair served as the butt of mean jokes. I was self-conscious and wanted so desperately to fit in, to look like everyone else with their straight hair, styled in ways I could only ever dream of. I learned patience when my mom would blow dry my hair, pulling down my curls to tame and control them, then douse them with obscene amounts of hairspray to prevent frizz. In actuality, these efforts were in vain. I could never truly escape the halo of frizz that the slightest touch of humidity, perspiration, or moisture would create.

We all have a natural desire to belong. In fact, this is an area of study that has been heavily researched. This ability plays an important role in psychological health and well-being. A person's ability to make choices and manage their own life is referred to as self-determination (Lavigne, Vallerand, and Crevier-Braud 2011).

Self-determination is connected to a person's sense of control they have over their choices and lives. It is also related to one's level of motivation because people are more motivated when they feel their efforts will influence the outcome. This need to belong is so deeply rooted in our psyche that any threat of rejection is said to have a similar reaction to that of physical pain (Laslocky 2013)

When you're motivated by internal sources, this is referred to as intrinsic motivation and is also the primary focus of self-determination, whereas external motivations, such as money or "things," is extrinsic motivation. In order to grow psychologically, a person needs to feel a sense of autonomy, competence, and connection. This connection or relatedness is what factors into how a person senses they belong or connect with other people (Cherry 2022).

If you've ever been in a relationship where you have considered walking away instead of putting the necessary work into making it last, only to find that you stayed, this is likely because of the notion of finding yourself in a constant state of seeking conflicts with our fundamental need to belong. Anxiety, depression, jealousy, and loneliness can result from a person sensing a threat that might impact a social attachment (Baumeister and Leary 1995, p. 503)

Self-determination plays a role in the workplace in terms of how people function in the real world. When they feel a sense of control, they are more likely to be committed and satisfied with their work. Likewise, if a person feels intrinsically motivated, they are more interested and passionate about what they do. Feeling like what they're doing is making a positive impact is often more engaging and motivational than rewards or external motivators.

The Daniel Pink Motivation Theory is a concept introduced in the book *Drive: The Surprising Truth About What Motivates Us*, by Daniel Pink. Pink argues that organizations and organizational leaders should adopt a new self-determination approach to motivation that focuses on desire to be autonomous, self-determined, and connected. He highlights the importance of three elements of intrinsic motivation: autonomy, mastery, and purpose (Pink 2017).

Daniel Pink explains autonomy as the desire to lead your own life. For children, this means playing and discovering things independently. While contrary to the traditional vision of management, he found that cultivating autonomy in the workplace to be effective, as employee autonomy ensured they were more invested in what they were doing. Four factors that impact employee autonomy are: time, technique, team, and task. For example, organizations such as Google, that give employees the freedom at work to spend their time on what they want to do, has led to increased ideas and innovations. This builds a stronger sense of autonomy.

Mastery is the desire to improve something that matters, and purpose is about the desire to serve something for a greater good. Pink suggests that leaders match tasks that suit the person's capacity but also to give them space and support to promote improvement and growth. Regarding purpose, he says joining a cause that is "bigger" than yourself drives the deepest motivation possible and unlocks the highest potential, even for complex problems.

Pink found that the traditional beliefs—the so-called "carrot and stick" method—still widely used to inspire motivation (both professionally and personally) had many shortcomings. While rewards and punishment have been found to be effective in certain situations, there are major drawbacks in the workplace. Financial incentives, for example, have not been found to improve employee performance and can in fact lead to less productivity. For simple task-oriented projects, rewards can be effective. In our world today, where corporate roles involve creative and conceptual thinking, rewards hinder motivation such as employee focus on the financial goal and can interfere with rather than inspire motivation. Autonomy, purpose, and mastery empower the employee and provide a degree of independence and control over their own domain, so long as employees have the necessary resources to make effective decisions. This results in higher productivity and a better quality of work.

Managers can foster and cultivate this sense in the office by providing meaningful feedback, showing support, and encouraging employees to take an active role.

When we're young, our curiosities lead us to explore and experiment so we can grow and develop into the person we are meant to be. Part of that exploration involves a willingness to rebel. If you have children, you've likely had experience with rebellious behavior to varying degrees at different stages. As a parent, allowing a child the freedom to safely rebel is the key. Rebellion gives way to a voice and a willingness to be vulnerable through exploration. To be honest, maybe I'm old, but it feels like there's far less rebellion in today's society as everyone works to what feels like conformity to ascend and belong versus rebel and stand out. We have far more acceptance today, and perhaps that's why rebellion doesn't seem as edgy. Nonetheless, bear in mind there's no one right way to do anything. No perfect formula or secret sauce. A little rebellion against what you're told is the "right way" to do, say, or act is, in my opinion, the start of your listening to your inner voice and trusting yourself. This is the secret sauce if there is one (Campbell 2015).

"A 'Creative Rebel' is a creative person who does things in their own way instead of following what everybody else says. It is not the one who makes noise or draws attention to themselves, but the one who remains steadfast and true to themselves," Violeta Nedkova said (Nedkova 2017).

You can't create without listening to your inner voice. Whether it's a painting or recognizing a solution to a problem, not paying attention to your inner voice makes it impossible to know what you want to create. In fact, I would suggest that, when you confirm and don't listen to the inner critic, you are creating your own creative block, fostered by the inner critic touting mental reminders of "should have, would have, or could have."

If you've ever felt flutters in your stomach when you're trying something new or maybe a bit of an anxious rush when you take a risk, you have felt what is sometimes called creative tension. An innovator might feel this when crafting new solutions for problems their customers may not even be aware of yet.

Thomas Jefferson once said, "If you want something you have never had, you must be willing to do something you have never done." In our personal and professional lives, most people try to avoid this feeling, but it's this avoidance that prevents ideas. Great ideas are found from pushing to the edges, not on the path of least resistance.

Instead, step into discomfort, break the rules, and own them. Embrace your inner rebel and ascend into elevated creativity that brings you personal satisfaction, peace, and mindfulness. Listen to your inner voice and do what works for you and what you're being pulled to do.

"To be creative and to get lost in creativity, you need a sort of calm content sense of peace about you. You need to be able to set all your worries aside and step into that magical relaxed state where the ideas flow" (Giles 2017).

If your creativity is feeling lackluster or stifled, you may be a candidate for imposing some structure or personal challenges to push your mind, but get rid of all those "should have, would have, or could haves" and remind yourself that creativity, as with life, is a process and a journey. Don't measure your outcomes as a validation of success. That's a crutch to justify insecurity. Being a rebel is not some sort of activist or revolutionary who changes the world and breaks rules on a daily basis. A creative rebel is a person who looks beyond superficiality and into the depths of their being to carve their own path, one who chooses to live life on their own terms and within their own rules. A creative rebel is authentic, lives with no regrets, lives fearlessly despite recognizing obstacles, and push ahead focused on owning their voice. They are leaders, not followers. Creative rebels recognize their superpower is their creativity, and they shamelessly own it to carve their path.

"To be a creative rebel also means to make bold life-affirming decisions that go against the grain" (Barth 2022).

In her book, *The Painting Path*, Linda Novick reminds the reader that artists have helped the world see things differently or in new ways. She explains a deep knowing often felt when one recognized something profound in what might be viewed as ordinary (Novick 2007). In fact, one statement I have included in my art bio is that I like to see the extraordinary in the ordinary. Like when you're driving down the road at dusk and see an incredible sunset along the highway, do you take the time to fully absorb and appreciate that sight? To me, this is part of being a creative rebel—seeing things differently and being okay with sharing them so others can see too.

KEY
TAKEAWAYS
Chapter 11

- Self-determination is connected to a person's sense of control they have over their choices and lives. It is also related to one's level of motivation because people are more motivated when they feel their efforts will influence the outcome. This need to belong is so deeply rooted in our psyche that any threat of rejection is said to have a similar reaction to that of physical pain (Laslocky 2013)

- Self-determination plays a role in the workplace in terms of how people function in the real world. When they feel a sense of control, they are more likely to be committed and satisfied with their work.

- Rebellion gives way to a voice and a willingness to be vulnerable through exploration.

- "To be a creative rebel also means to make bold life-affirming decisions that go against the grain" (Barth 2022).

- Break the rules and go where others don't. When someone tells a rebel they can't do something, rebels will go out of their way to prove them wrong.

- Reject the status quo. Be a disruptor.

What can you do?

Great ideas are found from pushing to the edges, not from the path of least resistance. What are some great ideas you've had, how did it make you feel to share them with others?

Think of friends you feel comfortable enough to share your ideas with. Consider them as your personal soundboard to bounce ideas off of. Doing so helps workout your idea so you can iterate. This will help boost your confidence.

Go out into the world today and try one new thing. It could be a daring new recipe, a new hairstyle, a different outfit, or a new place to go. You can chat with someone new or try a different way of doing things. Be bold and curious! Then, after you return from your adventure, write about it here. What did you do? How did it make you feel?

CHAPTER 12

SELF-ACCEPTANCE

There's an awkward feeling I often have when someone gives me a compliment. Certainly, I feel flattered by their words, but there's an odd feeling of resistance that accompanies that gratitude for their appreciation of my gifts. I've pondered this and have concluded that this complex multi-faceted emotion is rooted in an internal conflict.

This bubbling up of resistance to a compliment is my inner voice emerging to judge and sabotage my self-esteem. It's the wrench that's thrown to stifle my self-acceptance and break my creative expression.

Most people I know were told as children not to brag. Especially as a young girl, I was reminded that boastful behavior is unflattering and told that if I was good at something, people would compliment me and I would not need to tell them.

While I realize this came with every good intention, it certainly contributed to second-guessing my value. It seems that this, in turn, prompted me to become a harsh judge of my failures that resulted from creating impossibly high standards and masking my accomplishments. Once I realized this pattern, I was able to slowly and thoughtfully unlearn some of the limitations that prevented me from fully accepting all the parts of my being, including the creative side, which had been woefully neglected once I entered the professional phase of my life.

This is not an easy process, but it's a necessary step to owning your creative genius. Learning to fully accept yourself and take a compassionate and more loving stance toward yourself liberates your mind and renews your soul because it allows you to step forward into your power. By doing so, you treat yourself more kindly as your heightened self-worth inspires a deeper belief that you deserve to be authentically you and happy. Thus, you're more likely to honor your dreams, hopes, and aspirations and cultivate a life with purpose by living in your full potential.

Can you recall a time when you were young and you created something you shared with someone, only to feel judged when you shared it? That inner critic and judgment is the creativity killer that stifles expression. According to a recent study, education and creativity are interrelated, and motivation is regarded as a factor influencing creativity. There seems to be a connection between creative achievements and one's perceptions about oneself, including self-acceptance. The creativity of students increases along with their educational motivation to learn (Mostafavi et. Al 2020).

When you feel the inspiration to create something, or the seed of an idea pops into your head, do you snuff it out when you hear your inner critic evaluate your creation, or do you pursue the expression "feeling" as you go and open to exploration?

The latter comes when you are receptive and open to yourself. When you have a willingness to "be" and allow yourself the freedom to play, you'll become more mindful to your senses and creativity will come through. Giving yourself permission to be open to following the road where it leads prevents the negative thoughts that squash inspirations. Surely you might still have an inner thought that questions your idea, but, at the moment when deciding whether or not to pursue it, your openness will essentially prevent a block from stifling the inspiration.

We all have creative blocks, but it's the ability to identify and silence the critic by willingly asserting your power of self-acceptance that drives a conviction to prevent and release a creative block.

The Artist's Way, by Julia Cameron—a must-read for every creative—provides wonderful examples of how creative people have overcome their barriers through identifying the critical "voices from their past" that continue to occupy space in their heads and affect their feelings and actions (Cameron 2016).

One of the key things is to continue creating—writing, painting, and more. Don't wait until things are perfect to begin. Just start wherever you're at.

I have established routines in my life to ensure I'm taking the time for the things that are important to me beyond family or work. Using a bullet journal, my organizational method combines both an opportunity for creativity and insurance for maintaining a high degree of organization in a challenging world. Every Sunday, I plan for my week. This system is very fluid and without limitations, so it allows me to work within the space I need as opposed to a predesigned notebook or calendar.

Every month, a group of women and I meet virtually through an online community I've created to share a working session where we plan for the month ahead. It keeps us accountable and develops a habit. We share suggestions and stories. Similarly, with my fine art, I try to schedule time in my week to paint or create in an artistic and fluid manner verses the traditional creative demands associated with work. I find this schedule helpful for exercise as well, as it's built into my day to wake up at 5:00 a.m. and do yoga, meditate, and pray before I hop into work mode.

Another aspect of the relationship between self-acceptance and creativity is that when you genuinely accept yourself and thereby your expressions, you develop an openness to spontaneity. You must be able to start without a plan, or if you start with one to throw it away in between. Confidence and willingness to openness inspires thoughts and ideas to bubble up.

We all have flaws, and when we embrace our imperfections, we create power to receive insights, sparks of inspiration, and nuggets of wisdom. We cannot sense anything if we numb ourselves to the drug of judgment and self-criticism.

This is true whether you're composing a song, developing a new product, or solving a problem at work. When you are able to comfortably and confidently navigate and adapt to our ever-changing and demanding environment with a sense of mastery over your domain, you are functioning with a high degree of self-esteem. In so doing, you can work through and accept the problems that arise in everyday living with a mindset of knowing you will find a way to work through whatever comes your way to give yourself the best chance of making it through.

When you have this cool confidence that comes with high self-esteem, you're able to see things from different angles and use information in new, unusual, and unexpected ways to craft ideas or solve problems. You'll also have a higher degree of perseverance, and you'll accept failure not as rejection but rather as data intelligence that is part of the process. This openness to failure allows you to be creative in exploring alternatives and preventing you from giving up. It encourages experimentation, iteration, and discernment that allows you to suspend a need for external validation. You begin to see mistakes not as judgments but as opportunities.

Further, if you don't value yourself, it's unlikely you will dedicate the time and energy to living a healthier and more positive lifestyle. So, learning to truly care about yourself and honor your well-being is necessary for living up to your potential.

Love is like a garden we need to fertilize and cultivate. To fully give and receive love, we must first pull the weeds that sabotage it. We ward off invading pests in the form of toxic relationships and welcome animals that protect and help our garden grow (Lancer 2020).

Here are a few ways to help you cultivate a loving and caring relationship with yourself:

1. Learn to say no so you're not taking on too much that you're unable to produce the quality of work that would make you proud so that, in turn, you can enjoy what you must do.

2. Take time to be. Just sit and listen and observe. We need downtime, and you will feel better when you learn how to be by yourself and feel filled.

3. Get comfortable with failure. Lean into setbacks and use them to learn and grow—turn a negative into a positive. Don't let yourself muddle in negative feelings or emotions. That bad energy is toxic and will stop you from creativity and health and wellness.

4. Be grateful to be alive.

5. Always have a passion or a goal you can work toward that feeds your purpose.

KEY
TAKEAWAYS

- Resistance to a compliment is the inner voice emerging to judge and sabotage self-esteem. It's the Obstacle Monster that's resurfacing to stifle self-acceptance and break creative expression.

- Self-acceptance is a necessary step to owning your creative genius.

- Learning to fully accept yourself and take a compassionate and more loving stance toward yourself liberates your mind and renews your soul because it allows you to step forward into your power.

- When you are able to comfortably and confidently navigate and adapt to our ever-changing and demanding environment with a sense of mastery over your domain, you are functioning with a high degree of self-esteem. In so doing, you can work through and accept the problems that arise in everyday living with a mindset of knowing you will find a way to work through whatever comes your way to give yourself the best chance of making it through.

- Confidence and willingness to openness inspires thoughts and ideas to bubble up.

What can you do?

Self-acceptance means you simply give yourself a pass for your faults and weaknesses and stop trying to change them.

Acknowledging your failures and weaknesses is the only way you can begin to work on them and create real progress.

Make a list of your failures and weaknesses. Forgiveness and compassion are key to developing self-acceptance.

Think of your past self as a different person, and that you can only change what you can control right now, which is your present self.

Take a moment to write three positive affirmations to yourself below based on the voice of your inner critic to revert whatever they are saying. If your inner critic voice tells you "I am a failure," you can write down your successes.

CREATIVITY IN BUSINESS

Creative solutions are what differentiate one business from another and one product from the next, and they're what gives a company a competitive edge or product an unparalleled user experience. It's creativity that propels a company's success.

In fact, company leaders agree. According to executives surveyed by Forrester Research, 82 percent believe companies benefit from creativity with specific benefits, including increased revenue and greater market share. Further, 58 percent of respondents said they set goals around creative outcomes, and another 48 percent claim to fund new ideas spun out of creative brainstorming (Landry 2017).

While these statistics point clearly to a value and benefit for fostering a creative workplace, a major disconnect in the study results was that 61 percent of executives don't see their companies as creative.

A survey by IBM of more than 1,500 chief executive officers ranked creativity as the number one factor for future business success—above management discipline, integrity, and even vision (IBM 2010).

Creativity is an asset for both business and life that opens the door to big ideas or new opportunities. It requires both ingenuity and originality. Innovation is often clumped together with creativity as if the words are interchangeable, yet creativity should be viewed as a separate concept, more as a vehicle to move toward innovation. Innovation, on the other hand, requires skills from a variety of disciplines to realize an idea. A person can have terrific ideas and not be innovative. Creativity drives innovation.

"Why is this relationship between *creativity* and *innovation* important? Because it is impossible to develop a truly innovative organization if creativity is ignored or stifled. And likewise, without effective processes in place to transform creative ideas into practical, real world, value-added application, creativity is of no commercial value whatsoever" (SmartStorming 2018).

"But here is the secret: *Anyone* can be an innovator or creator, regardless of field or occupation. Scientists and engineers developing new applications of technology are innovators, but so is the marketing professional who finds a new way to reach customers, or the grocery store clerk who devises a system to extend the shelf life of produce. The concept of innovation has been locked inside a technology-shaped box, even though innovation *really* means using one's unique experiences to inspire new ways of thinking and doing. Innovation is identifying a challenge and finding a tailored, situationally specific way to overcome it. It involves observing the world and finding a new way to represent or analyze it. In other words, innovation requires all the imagination and ideation characteristic of creativity. But first we need to change the narrative about who 'qualifies' as a creator or innovator." The answer: everyone (Paris 2021).

"There may be no universal understanding of creativity. The concept is open to interpretation from artistic expression to problem-solving in the context of economic, social, and sustainable development. Therefore, the United Nations designated 21 April as World Creativity and Innovation Day to raise the awareness of the role of creativity and innovation in all aspects of human development" (United Nations 2021).

"Stifling creativity—or just failing to encourage it, for that matter—is dangerous in today's competitive business climate that rewards agility and punishes hesitancy. And as creativity and engagement work in tandem, inhibiting one may throttle the other" (Wigert and Robison 2018).

The first step toward increasing creativity in business is senior leadership recognizing creativity as a priority. Adopting a creative mindset lends to more comfort with ambiguity. Eight in ten CEOs surveyed said they expect their industry to become significantly more complex, while only 49 percent feel confident their organizations are equipped to deal with the transformation (IBM 2010). What's more is, despite the purported value companies place on creativity, few treat it like a job expectation and incorporate it into their performance development system. It's difficult to measure or assess something that doesn't have a dollar value. It's likely this reason that leaders are hesitant to implement creative programs into their organization.

In fact, a recent Gallup study of more than 16,500 employees shows that the three foundational factors needed to foster creativity in the workplace are all too rare:

- Expectations to be creative at work;

- Time to be creative; and

- Freedom to take the risks necessary to be creative (Wigert and Robison 2018).

As a result, businesses are missing an opportunity to foster growth.

"An ideal organization is one in which each worker's potentialities find room for expression" (The Age of Ideas 2022).

So now that we've recognized the value of creativity in the workplace, the question is, how does a leader foster creativity?

"'Innovate or die' is the battle cry of dozens of start-up founders and corporate executives trying to lead change in the modern era. Those who don't take risks and try new approaches are doomed to fall the way of Blockbuster and Blackberry."

Adopting a creative culture in your organization isn't about just doing a one-off art-inspired team-building activity and then never doing anything creative again. It's about embracing creative culture at all levels of the organization, all of the time.

Cultivating a creative culture begins with the HR department. Looking beyond experience and instead at people from different backgrounds or with different experiences will be more likely to challenge pre-existing beliefs and envision different solutions. You can't expect your company to move forward if you keep hiring the same people to do the same work.

Scott E. Page, a Leonid Hurwicz Collegiate professor at The University of Michigan, argues against hiring the "best" teams because they tend to develop the least creative results.

"Ranking people by common criteria produces homogeneity," he writes. "And when biases creep in, it results in people who look like those making the decisions. That's not likely to lead to breakthroughs."

"Employees with similar backgrounds and career paths tend to have the same perspective, limiting the variety of views in your organization." Instead, recognize the value of professionals who are flexible and creative, less "set in their ways" and willing to think out of the box.

To a conventional organization, hiring creatives can feel like you're bucking the system and going against the grain. And it is... in a good way. These are people who aren't afraid to share their ideas and are willing to challenge the status quo.

"Highly creative people tend to be rebellious," Jeffrey Baumgartner, author of *Anticonventional Thinking: The Creative Alternative of Brainstorming*, writes. "They think differently to averagely creative people, they tend to do things in unconventional ways, and they are not afraid to provoke others, including senior management."

One important detail to remember: If your company is willing to take the step to design a creative culture, hiring creatives is great, but leaders will also need to embrace the uncertainty and have a willingness to try some of their different ideas. If employee ideas are frequently rejected because leaders see them as risky or for fear of failure, they'll eventually stop coming to bosses with ideas. On the flip side, when you welcome and embrace the "out-of-the-box" ideas, your employees will be more likely to build on each other's creativity and push each other to come up with unique solutions. Doing this, especially in public at team meetings, will foster a creativity-positive workplace with existing team members where they feel their ideas are valued, not foolish. Allowing your employees the freedom to express their creativity has the power to challenge employees to reach goals and gives them space and autonomy to do so.

Jan Hoffmann-Keining, senior project manager at Retail Capital Partners, agrees. "Inspiring employees to work together and search for creative solutions isn't as easy as renovating the office and playing a company game of hot potato," he writes. "The changes that occur in your newly implemented creative culture need to be understood and supported by management, otherwise you will revert to old habits" (Guest User 2018).

For employees to feel commutable flexing their creative muscles, the organization should design an employee experience where workers feel invited to engage their creativity. They should start by working from top leadership down to embed their organization with a culture of creativity—starting with making creativity part of a person's job role. That means making observation, listening, thinking, and making connections—basic creativity—a factor in their performance development. When a person is fearful of taking risks or prohibited by a perceived barrier, they will not offer alternatives. Here are a few simple activities that can boost workplace creativity:

Regularly scheduled times allotted for creative endeavors. The discipline of scheduling creative time makes imagination a more accessible resource and helps to organize thoughts. The creative time elevates the value of creativity in an organization's culture as well as providing something tangible to measure, such as number of ideas, team participation, absenteeism, or job satisfaction.

A willingness to take risks is a critical element in the creative process, less competitive in the market, and slow to adapt to operational innovations that boost productivity, increase profit, aid retention, and improve recruitment.

Second, companies that discourage risk can create a climate of insecurity for their workers. Encouraging and motivating employees to move past their perceived limitations, and stepping beyond into uncertainty rather than staying within safety, can only be accomplished when leaders know the skills and motivations of their employees and set goals that are higher than current levels, but not so high as to cause frustration. The leaders must "raise the bar gradually and offer coaching and training to build skills that help people get over each new level" (Kouzes and Posner 2008, p207).

If you're a curious person willing to experiment and identify and solve problems, have you ever found yourself stifled by your manager? These are desirable traits in the workplace, yet more often than not, micromanagers prefer control, safety, and predictability, which hinders the qualities they are trying to develop. When management adopts more of an experimental and laboratory mentality, they can help foster more growth. Managers who support divergent thinking, or lateral thinking, are helping their team generate multiple creative solutions to the same problem.

Remote teams post-pandemic are commonplace. Without in-person interactions to bolster our professional relationships, there's more room to make negative—often unfounded—assumptions about our colleagues' behaviors. Trust is one of the most key elements needed to build effective teams. The lack of face-to-face interaction makes it more difficult to develop genuine relationships. To build trust, you must build transparency, as it shows your team they are trusted. This, in turn, makes them better informed, which will aid in their decision-making abilities.

You should ask for feedback and suggestions to help improve how you're communicating with your team and how your team is communicating and accessing information. This will offer engagement and encourage a problem-solving team-mind effort. Planning one-on-one meetings with staff gives them the opportunity to open up and build trust. When someone tells you the truth, withhold from any defensive response or you'll compromise the trust you built that prompted the feedback.

"Trust is built by spending time together, not necessarily around work-related tasks," says Scott Schieman, chair of the department of sociology at the University of Toronto's St. George campus. "We form and sustain social bonds this way, expressing verbal and nonverbal communication in ways that convey understanding, empathy, and shared concern. There is no way endless Zoom calls can replace the depth and quality of in-person human interaction" (Hickok 2021).

Take an interest in your team members' health and wellness. A team that is both physically and mentally healthy performs better, takes fewer sick days, and ultimately makes more money for the business.

Allow for a flexible schedule, as it can help reduce stress and improve team members' happiness with your team.

Create a wellness plan to support your team's well-being along with proving a wellness budget to use for healthy experiences like massages, gym memberships, or spa treatments. Creating a virtual retreat is another way to reward your team and create opportunities for social time with colleagues to help fuse your team together.

But that can also be a detriment to any business that prioritizes organic growth, likely costing the company more money by playing it safe because a certain level of controlled risk-taking and embracing failure are imperative for any organization to be successful.

"A company that isn't intentional and committed to this type of culture will ultimately inhibit growth—of its profits and of its people. But a company that promotes a culture of creativity accesses the full capacity of its workers, from imagination to engagement" (Wigert and Robison 2018).

KEY
TAKEAWAYS
Chapter 13

- Creativity is an asset for both business and life that opens the door to big ideas or new opportunities. It requires both ingenuity and originality.

- A person can have terrific ideas and not be innovative. Creativity drives innovation.

- Adopting a creative mindset lends to more comfort with ambiguity.
- Adopting a creative culture in your organization isn't about just doing a one-off art-inspired team-building activity and then never doing anything creative again. It's about embracing creative culture at all levels of the organization, all of the time.

- You can't expect your company to move forward if you keep hiring the same people to do the same work.

- When you welcome and embrace the "out-of-the-box" ideas, your employees will be more likely to build on each other's creativity and push each other to come up with unique solutions. This fosters a creative workplace.

What can you do?

Break the chains of your mind by encouraging people to seek out problems around them, either at work or home, then create out-of-the-box solutions.

The more we are aware of our external environment, the more we can recognize pain points which in turn can develop into opportunities if we allow ourselves to think different.

What are some pain points in your work or life you'd like to solve for?

What ideas do you have for alternative solutions?

The next time your team is struggling to come up with an idea or build trust, try this from IDEO. This activity is called, "List it Out."

"Choose a topic, like things people do in a bathtub or how to make driving more enjoyable. Give people in the room three to five minutes of heads-down time to list out everything they can think of. Share back ideas, making sure every person in the room gets to share at least one.

"Encouraging individual time to brainstorm instead of shouting out ideas helps include all the voices in the room, especially introverts. It also helps people get into the habit of sharing ideas quickly and deferring judg-ment until later" (Boyle 2020).

CREATIVE LEADERSHIP

"Creative leadership is a philosophy and an act: it develops and realizes innovative ideas through the shared ambition of improving the world through enterprise formation. Those who employ creative leadership do so by forging an environment that promotes creativity, innovation, and mission-driven entrepreneurship" (Djik, Davidson, and Mecozzi 2022).

Creative leadership involves using creative ideas to solve complex problems and changing situations. In today's changing and often chaotic environment, creative leaders are adept at managing change. Creative leaders are good for situations when morale needs to be changed and employees need flexibility to work on solving problems.

Empathy plays a key role in the philosophy of creative leadership by embracing change, motivating, and encouraging collaboration while maintaining an appreciation for the contributor's bravery and courage to stand by out-of-the-box ideas.

Managers who lead to fostering a creative workplace culture do so by building on qualities that drive both value and serve the triple bottom line, such as critical analysis, experimentation, collaboration, the art of taking bold actions balanced with calculated risk-taking, and an agility to be nimble in the face of change. Sharing many behaviors of entrepreneurs, creative leaders are oriented toward finding solutions to problems by tapping into inspiration from a variety of sources and disciplines. They think in terms of extremes and of life as a journey of learning and development. Recognizing patterns that reveal hidden opportunities, they process their domain both globally and strategically, driven toward their goals by a desire to act on big ideas.

Employees who are fortunate enough to work for creative leaders are inspired to work toward a common goal. These leaders are adept at inspiring the intrinsic motivation that enables the team members who work with them to feel like the work they are doing satisfies a deeper purpose and is helping them to reach their full potential.

Fostering a dialogue that invites the creation of ideas and solutions is two-way, and both parties—the idea generator and the leader who's judging the viability of the concept—need to function in an environment of mutual respect. Both need to recognize the relationship is symbiotic in that they need one another to grow, learn, process, ideate, and develop. Both sides must be aware of how they convey their feedback to promote growth and foster collaboration. Maintaining a demeanor of curiosity, coupled with criticism that facilitates growth by choosing words that validate an appreciation for the contri- bution while fostering a learning environment, ensures con- tinued team collaboration and allows the employee to adopt an attitude of knowing criticism is not personal and does not equate to failure but rather essential evolution.

As art students, courses have what's called a critique session built into the coursework. These are referred to as "crits," and nobody looks forward to these sessions. It's uncomfortable to pour your heart into an assignment and see it hanging on a wall with all the other students in the class, then, one-by-one, the instructor dissects each piece, providing insights, suggestions, and comparisons. I'm not going to lie—the first time is downright painful. At least it was to me. It made me feel raw, uneasy, and vulnerable. Much of the experience depends on the instructor, but it's somewhat of a rite of passage. It's something you hear about from other students too. "Wait until Professor Brown gets you in his crits session, he's tough!" Once you do it and put yourself in discomfort, if you allow yourself a willingness to learn and appreciate the experience, it's liberating. Being allowed to not take something personally comes with a feeling of freedom. You become a little more objective in looking at what you create when you don't take things personally. You realize it's not about you.

I mention this because, in my work, I have often come across a client who developed something for their business—say a website or brochure, for example—that they were especially proud of. When I became involved in an assessment of their brand and commented on that piece, I could feel their feathers begin to ruffle. I could feel their discomfort in my suggestions even though this person may not have any marketing or design experience. They were invested in what they created and felt challenged by any feedback. This has happened more than once, so I've learned how to gently caress the situation and ease into my feedback. It's almost as if some people revert to being a child and feel the parental or teacher criticism that makes them feel uncomfortable.

I think this is one reason why people are uncomfortable being creative. It's exactly why I feel everyone should go through a crit's session a few times in their lives. If you're in business and uncomfortable accepting personal feedback, then you'll either become reluctant to share your ideas, or you'll become defensive toward someone who gives you their opinion. Neither option is productive for any individual or team.

Not being able to take criticism is connected to a person's fear of failure. The problem is that not every negative comment is truly a failure or a win versus lose outcome. To me, it's more of a re-tool, realignment, or an evolution. All failures provide an opportunity to learn, resurrect drive, focus, and re-align. Regardless, the word isn't as important as the value of leadership that fosters a mindset of positivity, curiosity, resourcefulness, and confidence, so the ideas keep coming. Seeing fear as failure or as a definitive state or outcome truly hinders one's ability to see it as an opportunity for growth and improvement.

Eighty-six percent of businesses worldwide say developing new leaders is their organization's number one challenge, and only 15 percent are confident in their current leadership pipelines.

"Today's HR professionals and executives cite leadership development as a major human capital challenge and recognize that 'developing leaders within organizations is critical to business success.' As such, employers are seeking employees with leadership skills at all levels, from the CEO to individual contributors" (Doyle 2019).

"There are leadership experiences needed in virtually all aspects of business," says Rita Balian Allen, a Northeastern University lecturer and one of Boston Women's Business Journal's "Top Ten Executive Coaches." "Leadership isn't necessarily about managing. It's about having a vision and being able to influence people. It's taking an idea or a concept and bringing it alive. Everyone has the potential to unleash and nurture these skills."

Today's complex business world requires the use of different leadership styles to effectively manage their teams based on the needs of the organization. Five common leadership styles include:

1. Transformational leadership: These are influential leaders who are role models and inspire others by connecting with both the individual's sense of who they are and the organization's identity and vision. They are visionary and encourage critical thinking, creative problem-solving, and innovation. One impact of this style, according to the leadership studies scholars Bruce Avolio and Bernard Bass, who defined this term, is that this leadership style improves the morale and job performance of team members. Steve Jobs is an example of a transformational leader.

2. Participatory leadership: These are hands-on kind of leaders. They work to bring a more level playing field to management rather than a traditional top-down approach. This is a leader who views the employees as stakeholders in the organization, entitled to express their own voice. This type of leader purposefully engages and empowers employees who might be impacted by decisions to be part of the conversation. Participatory leadership is a very democratic approach with the needs of the employees as a priority. Former

Southwest Airlines CEO James F. Parker is a good example of this style of leadership.

3. Value-based Leadership: These are leaders who guide their teams by encouraging others to act in alignment with the organization's shared core values. They work to foster positive change by emphasizing the mission and purpose as opposed to solely on metrics. They are fully invested in the core values of the organization. This leader sets the foundation for how everyone in a company will engage and establishes an expectation that the leader will always operate for the greater good of all.

4. Situational leadership: This style was developed by business consultant and bestselling author Ken Blanchard and behavioral scientist Paul Hersey. It requires that the leader adjusts their management style to ensure they are leading in the most appropriate and successful way, thereby matching their behaviors to the performance needs of those they are working to influence. This style requires that they are nimble and willing to adapt, communicate in a clear and relatable manner, and have a keen understanding of when to change their leadership style depending on the business scenario—the situation. One example of a situational leader is former NBA Coach Phil Jackson, who managed his team based on their individual strengths, weaknesses, and motivations.

5. Servant leadership: These are leaders who are driven to build better organizations and a better, more

equitable world. This, in turn, enriches the lives of others. Robert K. Greenleaf first used this term to refer to a leader who consciously decides to work for and aspires to lead focused on other people's needs as their highest priority. This leader is not focused on personal or organizational power but is instead dedicated to sharing power and helping others grow and perform at their highest level as individuals and in their community. There have been many studies indicating organizations that are servant-led perform better and yield higher returns. Well-known advocates of this style of leadership include Ken Blanchard, Steven Covey, and Larry Spears.

In their book *The Leadership Challenge*, James Kouzes and Barry Posner studied hundreds of exemplary leaders and found there were five practices they shared. Effective leaders:

- Model the way: Create standards of excellence to set an example for others to follow.

- Inspire a shared vision: Show people the possibilities for the future.

- Challenge the process: Experiment and take risks to make meaningful improvements.

- Enable others to act: Actively empower people to strengthen the whole team.

- Encourage the heart: Celebrate the accomplishments of others (Kouzes and Posner 2008).

"Creative leadership is not industry-specific, nor is it one-size-fits-all. It is the individual act of a leader in the context of perpetual beta, and therefore path dependent. In contrast to analytical forms of leadership, where the act of problem-solving culminates in one truth, Creative Leadership presupposes that the drive for a solution to a problem or challenge can have several outcomes and is to a significant degree shaped by the leader" (Djik, Davidson, and Mecozzi 2022).

A few rules creative leaders might consider are:

1. Ideas come from all ranks and every team member can generate valuable and meaningful solutions to problems. Open the organization to diverse perspectives.

2. A creative leader doesn't need to be an artist or think of themselves as uber creative, but they must understand the creative process.

3. Create diverse teams with an emphasis on recognizing the strengths and weaknesses of their team so they can more easily identify areas they excel in and provide more opportunities for cultivating their strengths. This will position them in a role where they are successful.

4. Make building trust a priority along with providing clear goals and giving them freedom to make decisions.

5. Embrace failure and encourage your team to fail early so they can learn from it and iterate and try again.

6. Encourage and enable collaboration.

7. Create a process for filtering and eliminating ideas that are not working.

8. Maintain a spirit to motivate by allowing people to pursue their passions, ensuring projects are challenging and team members feel appreciated and valued.

9. Provide work that is viewed as meaningful, as people are more engaged when they view the works as for the better good or noble.

10. Be nimble.

11. Look for insights and ideas from unrelated fields, chance encounters, and the unexpected.

12. Get comfortable with contradicting insights, paradoxes, conflicting needs, and ambiguity.

13. Identify and challenge assumptions that underpin perceived realities.

14. Think in contrary directions and deliberately reject conventional, inherited parameters.

15. Don't be satisfied with the first solution but rather search for better concepts that bring major improvement.

16. View life as a journey where opportunities for learning and development are always present.

17. Think big, but with intention—focused on making an impact.

18. Be empathetic, aware of the connectedness of what's around you, mindful, and self-aware in the here and now. Be compassionate and humble with an openness to explore. Trust your intuition.

19. Look for team members who raise the caliber and diversity of the collective.

20. Be transparent and honest, exercising harmony between intentions, words, presence, and actions.

21. Work toward building an organizational culture that nurtures and cherishes the ideas of others, removes barriers, and structures incentives to reinforce the change that is being sought.

22. Provide the stories, experiences, and motivations that empower the organization toward a common goal.

23. Inspire people to act by creating a shared goal of working toward a better future.

24. Be bold in new areas and try not to be limited by what you know.

25. Embrace fears rather than avoiding them.

In today's complex and chaotic environment, leaders who can manage unpredictability and ambiguity are skills. Jon Kolko, founder of Austin Center for Design and author of *Creative Clarity: A Practical Guide for Bringing Creative Thinking into Your Company*, says, "Creativity is the key to addressing ill-formed business threats and for shaping poorly defined market opportunities." The problem, as he sees it, is most companies don't really know what creativity is, so they can't benefit from it, and when they try to inject creativity into new methodologies such as design thinking, the result is often chaotic (Naiman 2022).

Brian Arthur, known for his pioneering work in complexity economics at the Santa Fe Institute, states, "All great discoveries come from a deep inner journey. Leaders must intentionally pause and slow down to access a deeper level of knowing, which comes from inside yourself" (Naiman 2022).

When faced with a complicated dynamic situation that he is trying to figure out, he says, "I would observe, observe, observe, and then simply retreat. If I were lucky, I would be able to get in touch with some deep inner place and allow knowing to emerge. You wait and wait and let your experience well up into something appropriate. In a sense, there is no decision-making. What to do becomes obvious. You can't rush it. Much of it depends on where you're coming from and who you are as a person. This has a lot of implications for management. I am basically saying that what counts is where you're coming from inside yourself."

KEY TAKEAWAYS
Chapter 14

- Empathy plays a key role in the philosophy of creative leadership by embracing change, motivating, and encouraging collaboration while maintaining an appreciation for the contributor's bravery and courage to stand by out-of-the-box ideas.

- Managers who lead to fostering a creative workplace culture do so by building on qualities that drive both value and serve the triple bottom line, such as critical analysis, experimentation, collaboration, the art of taking bold actions balanced with calculated risk-taking, and an agility to be nimble in the face of change.

- Challenge the process: Experiment and take risks to make meaningful improvements.

- Embrace failure and encourage your team to fail early so they can learn from it and iterate and try again.

- Today's complex and chaotic environment leaders require the skills to manage unpredictability and ambiguity.

What can you do?

View failure as an opportunity to learn and grow.

Of the rules explained in this chapter for effective leaders, which do you feel are the most important?

Which rules would you benefit from working on to improve?

Reflect on the leaders you've worked with. Which skills did those you liked best possess?

Take a moment to think of either:

1. A recent challenge or a problem you solved, or

2. A fear you faced.

Now reflect on your role in the situation, how you could have improved upon it, or what you might have changed in retrospect. Write your thoughts here:

CHAPTER 15

A SPIRITUAL JOURNEY

We are all equipped with the potential for creativity, yet most people imagine great works of art, music, or amazing feats of humanity. This brings me to another aspect of creativity not discussed in business literature but often philosophized about: Is there a spiritual aspect to creativity?

These things may seem separate from spirituality, but they're not. After all, creativity plays an essential role in our lives by inspiring individuals to think about the world in different ways.

The lightbulb or spark of insight is usually associated with the stereotypical "aha" moment that comes when an idea arrives. We live in a left-brained society, which often downplays the power of creativity. While math and science are interesting and necessary, they don't have the power to open a person's heart and connect them to something deeper and spiritual the way creativity does. Regardless of your religious views, we can all agree that we're part of something greater than our fleshy bodies. Call it God or energy, or whatever you prefer, but we are all connected by this source of spirit. Creativity comes from within, and there's little you can do to influence it externally. This is precisely why it's essential to keep your inner voice functioning so you can be receptive and open to the spark that inspires creativity. This receptivity and openness are part of the mystery and likely the reason spirituality and creativity go hand in hand. It is a harmonious dance of positivity and guidance that cradles your being and drives you toward a creative journey.

"Spiritual intelligence is an all-encompassing form of intelligence. It includes the logical or intellectual aspects of your intelligence, as well as the emotional aspects. When you add spirituality to your intellectual views, you develop wisdom, peace, and creativity in your life" (Raising Self Awareness 2018).

Reflecting on a trip to New Mexico with my friend Christina, I recall how the new surroundings and inner freedom to explore inspired a deeply spiritual experience of awe and wonder. That, coupled with my own imagination and curiosity, created this deep desire to create. I felt pulled to take what had inspired this moment of peace and awe and move it from my mind to a canvas. It was an outpouring of wonder that I took from my soul and released it onto a canvas. Creativity springs from your soul.

This image of an electrically charged boom that takes a person from no idea to an explosive concept or creation is what you see in the movies and throughout mythology. It dates as far back to Plato and the Greeks. Plato referred to artists as people who imitated the reality God created, while the Greeks saw artists as divinely inspired and the result of some sort of mania or madness intertwined with spirit. Numerous stories throughout the ages support this notion of creativity as the lightbulb we associate with a spark of an idea. The problem is, when people associate creativity with a zap of genius, they are often led to give up their creative dreams thinking they don't have what it takes (Cameron 2013).

Let's look at how different religious and cultural views translate this idea of what creativity is.

Thinking of the ornate and beautiful churches, or the religious art throughout the ages—creativity has been used to depict the stories from the Bible and to echo the chambers with beautiful music.

Creativity in the Catholic Church is seen as the very essence of religion. The Bible's opening words are "In the beginning." It is a story of origins. Genesis is not a scientific account but rather a metaphor. It is imaginative and even playful, meant to be taken seriously but not literally. Much religion is about the poetics of life.

A few details to highlight:

- We call God our "Creator." And the Bible says He created humans "in His image" (to be like Him in character— Genesis 1:26). Therefore, in order to be in alignment with God's intended design for how we are to love, we would need to be "creating" at some level (Kolstad 2022).

- In the two narratives of Genesis:

  - Genesis 1:1-2:4, seven days: God "speaks" the world into being. It is a reminder of the power of words to create and heal, or to destroy and hurt.

- Genesis 2:4-3:24, garden of Eden: Adam and Eve, of the Tree of Life and the Tree of Knowledge of Good and Evil, is a more mythological story, intent on teaching us not the facts of creation but its purposes.

A movement to bring a modern renaissance to the Catholic Church has begun. One organization, Catholic Creatives, is committed to using their platform to sponsor initiatives that foster true good and beauty. According to their website, Catholic Creatives is a "movement of Catholic designers, filmmakers, photographers, creative thinkers, artists, entrepreneurs, and others working to bring the gospel to the world in fresh, beautiful ways." The organization also provides resources and opportunities for collaboration (Catholic Creatives 2023).

In the Jewish tradition, creativity is viewed as a birthright, and the Torah teaches that it is foundational to Judaism. A few details to highlight include (Allen 2022):

- The first five words of the Torah are *Beresheit bara Elohim*—"In the beginning, God created." Only a few verses later, we read that humans are created *b'tzelem Elohim* ("in the image of God").

- If God is, first and foremost, a creator, and we are created in God's image, then we, too, are created to be creators.

- Ancient rabbis knew activating creativity could be a powerful way to tap into our deepest selves and to access the Divine.

- After the destruction of the second temple, there were two pathways:

  - *Beit knesset*, or house of prayer

  - *Beit midrash*, the house of study

- Even though they rely on fixed text, it is radical creativity that is said to have fueled the spiritual and intellectual foundation of the work in both.

- "Creativity as a spiritual practice is a way for us to partner with God and to develop the character traits that allow us to stay in ongoing co-creative partnership."

The Jewish Studio Project (JSP) is an organization that "cultivates creativity as a Jewish practice for spiritual connection and social transformation." On the website, JSP is explains, "Creativity is the wellspring of our deepest power and among the best tools we have for exploring, adapting, and bringing forth new ways to thrive in our ever-changing world. Creativity is inherent within all of us, yet we live in a society in which most of us are cut off from this essential part of who we are. This is a crisis of spirit and imagination. Jewish Studio Project (JSP) exists to address this profound need."

The following is also from the JSP website and explains the steps of their methodology:

"First is spiritual grounding, where one begins by a blessing or personal sharing to encourage a connection to something bigger and beyond the self. Next is suggested group study, then intention setting, which involves writing a statement of what is hoped to be gained from the art making practice. Next is placing the intention aside to engage with the act of making art, using whatever sparks one's attention as a guide for where to begin. There is an emphasis on following awareness and what pleasure. Lastly is what JSP refers to as witnessing. They explain that by turning the attention and full consciousness to what is received from art making, this is how intention gets actualized. Things such as sitting quietly to reflect or write of the experience to witness the experience."

In Islamic studies, the main fundamentals of creativity are sincerity, conformity with the *shari'ah*, beneficial products, usage of lawful means, the ethical and moral system, *ijtihad* (independent legal reasoning), and rejection of imitation (Al Karasneh, Saleh, and Mohammad 2010).

A few details to highlight include:

- The study highlighted the Qur'anic methodology that enhances creativity among people.

- Islamic perspective of creativity: It is considered necessary to explain the conceptual meanings of this notion and its development in the Islamic heritage.

- Creativity in-depth and in a very systematic manner: It explained the main characteristics of the Islamic concept of creativity, such as its multi-faceted nature, as well as dealing with concrete issues and problems.

- Yousif, an Islamic author, created a methodology that the Qur'an in particular elaborated on the sources of inspiration, tools, and techniques as a help to understanding creativity from an Islamic perspective.

Buddhism has inspired many art objects created over the centuries, including statues, monuments, temples, icons, and so on. Some art forms, particularly Japanese ones, are considered no less than expressions of the enlightened mind. Many Zen Masters were known for their calligraphy, drawing, or poetic skills. The now famous music of shakuhachi flute was popularized by the fuke sect of Buddhism (Guruge 2010).

Buddhist practice requires not just moment to moment awareness but also considerable continuity of purpose. It's a belief that one can be creative, but it should be motivated by a selfless goal. It's not perhaps as much about expressing oneself as much as it is motivated by the need to learn to be selfless.

The focus in the journal article *Creativity in the Buddhist Perspective*, by Nolan Pliny Jacobson, is not on creative work in the arts and sciences but rather on "the creativity that transforms individuals and their experience by enriching the flow of quality and widening the range of their perceptive participation in the life of the world. The sense of our being individual and unrepeatable actualities in a world where new increments of quality are forever being added is "the gift of aesthetic significance" that frees us from the limitations of any one occasion that happens in our lives. The feeling of these increments of quality is the feeling of the basic and unavoidable change in the ongoing of a dynamic world. It is simply "the becoming of ever-new events."

I once read that faith is a dance between the mind, spirit, and experience. I'm not sure where I saw this, but it stuck with me. Religion can be a touchy subject for many people. There are pluses and minuses to everything—religion included. To me, it seems that in order to believe in a God, one must be open to imagining. All religions and faiths encourage opening our minds so we can see the beauty in both the scripture and the traditions, which, in turn, is meant to guide and ground us. Whether you meditate or are active in a particular belief, prayer and meditation have tremendous health benefits. Opening our minds and having a willingness to receive is a beautiful gift gained from tapping into our spiritual self and listening deeply to an inner knowing. Most spiritual leaders have written about their own mindful journey. Buddha, Hazrat Ibrahim (AS), Prophet Muhammad (P.B.U.H.), for example, all used to meditate and search the skies for answers. Allow your imagination the freedom to be open by sitting quietly and peacefully in a space where you can release your inner worries and let go. You'll be glad you did.

KEY
TAKEAWAYS
Chapter 15

- There a spiritual aspect to creativity as it inspires individuals to think about the world in different ways.

- Creativity comes from within.

- it's essential to keep your inner voice functioning so you can be receptive and open to the spark that inspires creativity. This receptivity and openness are part of the mystery and likely the reason spirituality and creativity go hand in hand. It is a harmonious dance of positivity and guidance that cradles your being and drives you toward a creative journey.

- Whether you meditate or are active in a particular belief, prayer and meditation have tremendous health benefits. Opening our minds and having a willingness to receive is a beautiful gift gained from tapping into our spiritual self and listening deeply to an inner knowing.

What can you do?

Most spiritual leaders have written about their own mindful journey.

- Say yes to accepting the voice of inspiration

- Find quiet moments of calm to just "be" so you are open to receiving the flow of brilliance in your life

- Use mindfulness and meditation to find peace and awaken your senses to the world around you.

What does the spiritual / creative connection mean to you?

"We can choose when to open to our creativity by choos-ing our intention. When our intention is to have control over getting love and avoiding pain, we close down and cannot access the gifts of Spirit. The intention to con-trol is the opposite of the intention to learn. When our intention is to learn about love and truth, our energy opens and creativity flows. Learning is a surrender of our illusions of control. Our choice to learn rather than control, and to move into and trust our imagination, opens us to the flow of creativity, as well as to the love, peace, joy, and wisdom of Spirit. We all have the gift of creativity. When you let go of the illusion of control and open to learning, your unique gifts of creativity will flow through you" (Paul 2016).

In the space below, write an intention on why and how you would like to open yourself to creativity.

CONCLUSION

Whether you allow yourself the freedom to get lost in the sky or to feel a deeper inspiration from within, there is a place for you to find your creative voice. It's beautiful and powerful to embrace a creative awakening to feel renewed wonder and awe from what's surrounded you that you hadn't fully realized.

Like everything in life, though, it takes a little work to prevent the mindfulness from fading and prevent yourself from slipping back into old habits. In the workplace or your daily life, embracing creativity offers life a different lens as you hone your critical thinking skills that enable you to identify and solve problems more keenly aware.

From daydreaming to rebellion, accepting a life tapped into creativity is far from conventional in that you allow yourself to change the rules and live a more fulfilling life. True creativity and innovation comes from looking at things differently. The new perspective will propel your mind to a place of heightened awareness and deep awakening. As your mind takes a break, allow the subconscious an opportunity to bubble up and offer its contributions.

For organizations interested in excelling at problem-solving, it is essential to create an environment that cultivates creativity and innovation. By utilizing team and leadership strategies to engage employees in education and collaboration, efficiency and profitability in the workplace can increase, as well as job satisfaction.

There's also a deeply spiritual component to this process of creativity. Mindfulness, and an awareness of the world around you in a deeper and appreciative sense, is what causes you to have an imaginative spark that enables you to be creative. When an inner, more spiritual guide propels you to recognize a component of nature—the sky, the trees, an animal or insect—it also inspires you to be imaginative and contemplative with the desire that motivated you to create something. Establishing a meditation/mindfulness practice is a way to open up to the kind of creativity that leads to innovation.

Removing obstacles such as functioning from a place of fear and instead adopting an openness will help you access creative potential. You can do this by loving yourself, eliminating limiting beliefs, and removing judgments and the inner critic that sabotages and instead own who you are, so you can move forward fully embracing the person you have become and the path on your journey. This relinquishes you of your emotional burden and allows you to blossom—honestly and authentically.

Making sense of who we are helps us become who we were meant to.

As a fellow misfits in my own mind, I hope this book sparked and propelled you into liberating yourself from the chains of your discomfort and gave you the tools to embrace your inner creative genius.

Creativity is indeed a gift that needs to be fed. While it takes discipline and accountability, you are the only one who can control how you use your gifts or the meaning and value they afford you in the satiation they provide. This book was also meant to be an invitation to accept the reality of your amazingness. Don't wish you could contribute at work or in life in a creative way—embrace it. Don't deny yourself the opportunity to find clarity and peace in the stillness of your creative mind. You have a story. We all have a story. Think about how your story should go and journey into creativity to heed the call your personal truth can land on you. Be courageous and place a bet on your success—don't compromise. Love passionately and stand up for your ideas and dreams.

Shift your mindset to finding gratitude and simple things and look at failure as a means to reveal what you are good at and can succeed at. Don't get stuck on measurement as a bar of success. Stop expecting the outcome to be a success to the point of forgetting to enjoy what you're doing.

Intrinsic motivation involves performing a task because it's personally rewarding to you.

Extrinsic motivation involves completing a task or exhibiting a behavior because of outside causes, such as avoiding punishment or receiving a reward.

The main difference between intrinsic and extrinsic motivation is that intrinsic motivation comes from within and extrinsic motivation comes from outside. While both types of motivation are important, they have different effects on how you work.

Extrinsic motivation is beneficial in some cases. For example, working toward gaining a reward of some kind can be helpful when you need to complete a task you might normally find unpleasant.

Intrinsic motivation, however, is typically a more effective long-term method for achieving goals and completing tasks in a way that makes you feel fulfilled. While extrinsic motivation is helpful in certain situations, it may eventually lead to burnout or lose effectiveness over time.

Sometimes intrinsic and extrinsic motivation can work together to help you complete a task. For example, if you have a job and are working on completing a project, you might be extrinsically motivated to finish it to meet a teammate's timeline. You might be intrinsically motivated to finish it because you enjoy the project and want to do a good job.

Get rid of waste and decrease limitations that prevent you from accessing creativity. Make a secret with yourself to always be on a journey that's creatively inspired.

My dad took a risk, and in his blue-collar, working-class world, he didn't go to work in a factory. Instead, he pursued his life's passion—cars. He may not have followed the creative process in its entirety, but he did make the rules for himself and definitely was thinking outside the box. His determination, dedication, and willingness to find solutions to difficult challenges was inspirational. I would like to interview him about how he approached problems in his business. I bet he had to utilize creativity in the garage and as a developer.

Give yourself permission to take big chances; to believe you can take risks. Find a singular focus and clarity to see the details of things and moments around you that are meant for you to capture. Feel chosen and like you've been gifted. Enjoy the feeling of being pulled toward something that becomes so deeply meaningful it changes you. Be objective and remove yourself from projecting what you fear onto what you create.

KEY
TAKEAWAYS
Conclusion

- From daydreaming to rebellion, accepting a life tapped into creativity is far from conventional in that you allow yourself to change the rules and live a more fulfilling life. True creativity and innovation comes from looking at things differently. The new perspective will propel your mind to a place of heightened awareness and deep awakening. As your mind takes a break, allow the subconscious an opportunity to bubble up and offer its contributions.

- Removing obstacles such as functioning from a place of fear and instead adopting an openness will help you access creative potential. You can do this by loving yourself, eliminating limiting beliefs, and removing judgments and the inner critic that sabotages and instead own who you are, so you can move forward fully embracing the person you have become and the path on your journey.

- Give yourself permission to take big chances; to believe you can take risks.

- Creativity is a garden that needs to be fed.

What can you do?

Join our Judgement-Free Creative Space! Visit: facebook.com/groups/CreativeIQ

Want free swag to spark your creativity? Visit: ReneeMartinez.com/swag

Interested in having Renee speak at your next event, work with your team to boost their Creative IQ or help your organization adopt a creative culture? Visit: ReneeMartinez.com

Interested in 1:1 coaching, small group or custom retreat experiences to reclaim and recharge your Creative IQ? Visit: ReneeMartinez.com

ACKNOWLEDGMENTS

It's been quite a journey of highs and lows, new beginnings, and unexpected endings throughout the process of writing this book. *CreativeIQ* would not have been possible without the love and support of the many people I am lucky to call family and friends. There is no way this book would have been realized without your encouragement, guidance, interest, and support for sharing my voice. To you, I am forever grateful.

I'd like to start by thanking my family for walking by my side on this journey every step of the way, especially my four sons, who are a constant source of inspiration, love, and support, and Rod for sharing important years on the journey that led me to who I am today.

Next, thank you to my parents. To my mom for all the time spent at the kitchen table drawing with me and creating stories filled with laughter and creativity. To my dad, I miss your entrepreneurial spirit and problem-solving mind. To my brothers and friends.

Thank you to the people I had the pleasure of interviewing and to everyone who read, listened to, or brainstormed with me on anything related to *CreativeIQ*, I'm so grateful for your help to make this book the best it can be.

To Miss Turici, my high school art teacher, who understood my quirkiness and inspired me to do my best.

A special thank you to everyone who preordered a copy of my book and donated to my prelaunch campaign. I am grateful to have so many people in my life who love and support me.

Matt Armstrong	Katie Gardinier
Robert M Belan	Angela Garofalo
Jeffrey Bertrand	Karen Giacalone
Allison Blair	Ken Harrison
Nicole Bradley	Tripp Higgins
Kevin C. Brinkman	Edward Jenkins
Blake Carbone	Lisa Jeras
Seavon Chalmers	Venessa Johnson
Michael Colton	Dale Kates
Linda Crist	Sydney Kates
Nate Crowe	Kimberly Kemsley
Carrie Curran	Jennifer Kostowniak
Beth Embrescia	Kevin Kruszenski
Jason Falls	Alex Larence
Traci Felder	Lee J MacLeod
Sharon Fries	Sherri Markham
Lynda Gallagher	Gina Nicola

Richard Oliveri

Dale Pacovsky

Elizabeth Petruccelli

Candace Remington

Matt Rigerman

Frances Russo

Heather Russo

Robert Evan Styles

Mary Szarek

Andrea Todaro

Matthew Waz

Angela Wilcoxson

Jamie Wilmot

Doan Winkel

Yi Yeo

Mary Kay Yuhas

Susan Ziolkowski

Thank you to the team at New Degree Press. Thank you for providing a platform to bring my book to life. Eric Koester, Regina Stribling, Kathy Wood, Leila Summers, Linda Beradelli, John Saunders, Michelle Pollack, Kristy Carter, and Jordan Waterwash deserve special thanks. No one has done more to make this book happen, though, than Julie Colvin. A special thank you to Kehkashan Khalid for your kindness and steady commitment to keeping me accountable to myself and your constant reassurance. I am so grateful to have had you on my team.

APPENDIX

INTRODUCTION

Exploring Your Mind. 2020. "Yin and Yang: The Duality of Existence."
Exploring Your Mind. June 2020.
https://exploringyourmind.com/yin-and-yang-the-duality-of-existence/.

National Gallery of Ireland. 2022. "Mindfulness and Art." *Highlights of the
Collection* (blog), *National Gallery of Ireland.* 2022.
https://www.nationalgallery.ie/art-and-artists/highlights-collection/
mindfulness-and-art.

Sedacca, Matthew. 2019. "How Aging Shapes Narrative Identity." *Nautlius*,
August 2019.
https://nautil.us/how-aging-shapes-narrative-identity-237518/.

CHAPTER 1

Cuncic, Arlin. 2022. "What Is Imposter Syndrome?" *Verywell Mind*, November 2022.
https://www.verywellmind.com/imposter-syndrome-and-social-anxiety-
disorder-4156469.

Saripalli, Vara. 2021. "Imposter Syndrome: What it is & How to Overcome it."
Mental Well-Being (blog), *Healthline.* April 16, 2021.
https://www.healthline.com/health/mental-health/imposter-syndrome.

Sakulku, Jaruwan and James Alexander. 2011. "The Imposter Phenonmenon."
International Journal of Behavioral Science 6, no. 1 (2011): 75-97.

CHAPTER 2

Adobe. 2020. "Adobe Study Reveals Growing Importance of Creative Skills in
College Admissions." *Adobe Blog* (blog), *Adobe.* September 23, 2020.
https://news.adobe.com/news/news-details/2020/Adobe-Study-Reveals-
Growing-Importance-of-Creative-Skills-in-College-Admissions/default.aspx.

Association of Waldorf Schools of North America. 2015. "Waldorf Education: An Introduction." Waldorf Education. Accessed December 23, 2022. https://www.waldorfeducation.org/waldorf-education.

Bertagnoli, Lisa. 2022. "Divergent Thinking: What It Is, How It Works." *Career Development* (blog), *Builtin*. July 28, 2022. https://builtin.com/career-development/divergent-thinking.

Carr, Austin. 2010. "The Most Important Leadership Quality for CEOs? Creativity." *Fast Company*, May 2010. https://www.fastcompany.com/1648943/most-important-leadership-quality-ceos-creativity.

Cherry, Kendra. 2022. "Lev Vygotsky's Life and Theories." *History and Biographies* (blog), *Verywell Mind*. April 2, 2022. https://www.verywellmind.com/lev-vygotsky-biography-2795533.

Haberski, Ray. 2013. "The Origins of Creativity." *U.S Intellectual History Blog* (blog) *Society for U.S. Intellectual History*. June 7, 2013. https://s-usih.org/2013/06/the-origins-of-creativity/.

Jones, Stacey. 2022. "What is the Montessori Teaching Method?" *Montessori Method* (blog), *Montessori Today*. 2022. https://montessorifortoday.com/what-is-the-montessori-teaching-method/.

Kaufman, Peter. 2012. "Cram. Memorize. Regurgitate. Forget." *Social Institutions: Work, Education, and Medicine* (blog), *Everyday Sociology Blog*. April 26, 2012. https://www.everydaysociologyblog.com/2012/04/cram-memorize-regurgitate-forget.html.

Teaching Through Play. 2019. "Why is Play Important in Early Childhood." *Teaching Through Play,* June 2019. https://teachingthroughplay.com/why-is-play-important-in-early-childhood/.

University of Minnesota. 2022. "Sociology." University of Minnesota Libraries. Accessed December 23, 2022, https://open.lib.umn.edu/sociology/chapter/16-1-a-brief-history-of-education-in-the-united-states/.

Visual Paradigm. 2022. "Solving Problem Creatively with Concept Fan Technique." *Knowledge* (blog), *Visual Paradigm*. Accessed December 23, 2022. https://online.visual-paradigm.com/es/knowledge/problem-solving/problem-solving-with-concept-fan/.

CHAPTER 3

Advertising Row. 2021. "What are the 5 steps of the creative process?" *Advertising Magazine* (blog), *Advertising Row*. December 19, 2021. https://advertisingrow.com/advertising-magazine/what-are-the-5-steps-of-the-creative-process/.

Beaty, Roger, Mathias Benedek, Scott Kaufman, and Paul Silvia. 2015. "Default and Executive Network Coupling Supports Creative Idea Production." *Scientific Reports* 5, no. 10964 (June). https://doi.org/10.1038/srep10964.

Bloomsoup. 2021. "Open Monitoring Meditation: The Essential Guide." *Meditation* (blog), *Bloomsoup*. Accessed December 23, 2022. https://bloomsoup.com/open-monitoring-meditation/.

Boers, Elroy, Mohammad H. Afzali, and Patricia Conrod. "Temporal Associations of Screen Time and Anxiety Symptoms among Adolescents." *The Canadian Journal of Psychiatry*, 2019, 070674371988548. https://doi.org/10.1177/0706743719885486.

Colzato, Lorenza S., Ayca Szapora, Dominique Lippelt, and Bernhard Hommel. "Prior Meditation Practice Modulates Performance and Strategy Use in Convergent- and Divergent-Thinking Problems." *Mindfulness* 8, no. 1 (2014): 10–16. https://doi.org/10.1007/s12671-014-0352-9.

Gannett, Allen. 2018. *The Creative Curve: How to Develop the Right Idea at the Right Time*. Danvers, MA: Currency.

Gilbert, Elizabeth. 2009. "Your Elusive Creative Genius." Filmed 2009 Long Beach, CA. TED video, 19:15. https://www.ted.com/talks/elizabeth_gilbert_your_elusive_creative_genius.

Kaufman, Scott. 2014. "The Messy Minds of Creative People." *Beautiful Minds* (blog), *Scientific American*. December 24, 2014. https://blogs.scientificamerican.com/beautiful-minds/the-messy-minds-of-creative-people/#.

Kelley, Tom. 2001. *The Art of Innovation: Lessons in Creativity from IDEO, America's Leading Design Firm*. Danvers, MA: Currency.

Lochhead, Lisa. 2021. "A New Year Prayer: 7 Reflection Points for Wholeness and Well-being." *Connect* (blog), *Lisa Lochhead*. Accessed December 23, 2022. https://www.lisalochhead.com/blog/new-year-prayer-2021.

Universiteit Leiden. 2012. "Meditation makes you more creative." *Science News* (blog), *Science Daily*. April 19, 2012. https://www.sciencedaily.com/releases/2012/04/120419102317.htm.

CHAPTER 4

Association for Psychological Science. 2010. "Eye Movements Reveal Readers' Wandering Minds." *Latest Research News* (blog), *Association for Psychological Science*. August 30, 2010. https://www.psychologicalscience.org/news/releases/eye-movements-reveal-readers-wandering-minds.html.

Baos, Gary. 2016. "The Neuroscience of Paying Attention or Not." *News* (blog), *Athinoula A. Martinos Center for Biomedical Imaging.* February 14, 2016. https://www.nmr.mgh.harvard.edu/news/20160214/neuroscience-paying-attention-or-not.

Fink, Andreas, Ronald H. Grabner, Mathias Benedek, Gernot Reishofer, Verena Hauswirth, Maria Fally, Christa Neuper, Franz Ebner, and Aljoscha C Neubauer. 2009. "The creative brain: investigation of brain activity during creative problem solving by means of EEG and FMRI." *National Library of Medicine* 30, no. 3 (March): 734-48. doi: 10.1002/hbm.20538.

Georgia Institute of Technology. 2017. "Daydreaming is good: It means you're smart." *Science News* (blog), *Science Daily.* October 24, 2017. https://www.sciencedaily.com/releases/2017/10/171024112803.htm.

Lehrer, Jonah. 2012. *Imagine: How Creativity Works.* Boston, MA: Houghton Mifflin.

Stop Maladaptive Daydreaming. 2022 "The Differences Between Mind Wandering and Maladaptive Daydreaming." *Maladaptive Daydreaming Blog* (blog), *Stop Maladaptive Daydreaming.* October 10, 2022. https://maladaptivedaydreaming.org/blogs/md/mind-wandering.

Zedelius, Claire. 2020. "Daydreaming Might Make You More Creative—But It Depends on What You Daydream About." *Behavioral Scientist*, November 2020. https://behavioralscientist.org/daydreaming-might-make-you-more-creative-but-it-depends-on-what-you-daydream-about/.

CHAPTER 5

Association of Waldorf Schools of North America. 2015. "Waldorf Education: An Introduction." Waldorf Education. Accessed December 23, 2022. https://www.waldorfeducation.org/waldorf-education.

Education Northwest. 2010. "What Teachers Need to Know About the Common Core State Standards." *Teaching Reading*(blog), *Reading Rockets.* 2010. https://gsas.harvard.edu/news/stories/imposter-syndrome.

Failure Lab. 2021. "The Backstory." Failure Lab. Accessed December 23, 2022. https://www.failure-lab.com/backstory.

Kim, Kyung Hee. 2011. "The Creativity Crisis: The Decrease in Creative Thinking Scores on the Torrance Tests of Creative Thinking." *Creativity Research Journal* 23, no. 4 (November): 285-95. https://doi.org/10.1080/10400419.2011.627805.

Siltanen, Rob. 2011. "The Real Story Behind Apple's Think Different Campaign." *Forbes*, December 2011. https://www.forbes.com/sites/onmarketing/2011/12/14/the-real-story-behind-apples-think-different-campaign/?sh=2653604c62ab.

Yun, Jackie. 2018. "Imposter Syndrome." *News* (blog), *Harvard University.* February 26, 2018. https://gsas.harvard.edu/news/stories/imposter-syndrome.

CHAPTER 6

Airfocus. 2022. "Glossary." Airfocus. Accessed December 23, 2022. https://airfocus.com/glossary/what-is-divergent-thinking/.

Boitnott, John. 2019. "What Are SMART Goals and How Can You Set and Achieve Them?" *Entrepreneur,* November 2019. https://www.entrepreneur.com/leadership/what-are-smart-goals-and-how-can-you-set-and-achieve-them/342898.

Boudreau, Emily. 2020. "A Curious Mind." *Usable Knowledge* (blog), *Harvard Graduate School of Education.* November 24, 2020. https://www.gse.harvard.edu/news/uk/20/11/curious-mind.

Cherry, Kendra. 2022. "What is Mindfulness Meditation." *Meditation* (blog), *Verywell Mind.* September 22, 2022. https://www.verywellmind.com/mindfulness-meditation-88369.

Cherry, Kendra. 2022. "What Mindset is and Why it Matters." *Cognitive Psychology* (blog), *Very Well Mind.* September 20, 2022. https://www.verywellmind.com/what-is-a-mindset-2795025.

Csikszentmihalyi, Mihaly. 1996. *Creativity: The Works and Lives of 91 Eminent People.* NY: Harper Collins.

Dweck, Carol S. 2007. *Mindset: The New Psychology of Success.* NY: Ballantine Books.

Dyer, Jeff, Hal Gregersen, and Clayton M. Christensen. 2011. *The Innovator's DNA: Mastering the Five Skills of Disruptive Innovators.* Boston, MA: Harvard Business Review Press.

Herrity, Jennifer. 2022. "How Do You Set SMART Goals? Definition and Examples." *Career Development* (blog), *Indeed.* July 2, 2022. https://www.indeed.com/career-advice/career-development/smart-goals.

Murphy, Mark. 2018. "Neuroscience Explains Why You Need To Write Down Your Goals If You Actually Want To Achieve Them." *Forbes,* April 2018. https://www.forbes.com/sites/markmurphy/2018/04/15/neuroscience-explains-why-you-need-to-write-down-your-goals-if-you-actually-want-to-achieve-them/?sh=4295a7a27905.

Posture. 2020. "The Mentality of Creativity." *News* (blog), *Posture.* October 6, 2020. https://www.getposture.com/the-mentality-of-creativity/.

Wordnik. 2009. *Mindset.* Portland: Wordnik. https://www.wordnik.com/words/mindset.

CHAPTER 7

Art Therapy. 2022. "Reflecting on Edith Kramer: Art Therapy Pioneer and Artist." *Featured* (blog), *Art Therapy.* June 25, 2022. http://www.arttherapyblog.com/featured/reflecting-edith-kramer-art-therapy-pioneer-artist/#.Y6q_NiORpNo.

Brown, Stuart, and Christopher Vaughan. 2009. "Play: How it Shapes the Brain, Opens the Imagination, and Invigorates the Soul." *Books* (blog), *National Institute of Play.* 2009. https://www.nifplay.org/books/play-how-it-shapes-the-brain-opens-the-imagination-and-invigorates-the-soul/.

Csikszentmihalyi, Mihaly. 2008. *Flow: The Psychology of Optimal Experience.* NY: Harper Perennial Modern Classics.

Landers, Cassie. 2022. "New Research Underscores the Power of Play-Based Learning." *Viewpoint* (blog), *The Subir & Malini Chowdhury Center Institute for South Asia Studies, UC Berkeley.* October 13, 2022. https://chowdhurycenter.berkeley.edu/new-research-underscores-power-play-based-learning.

Malchiodi, Cathy. 2006. *Art Therapy Sourcebook.* NY: McGraw Hill.

Marais, Saya Des. 2022. "The Importance of Play for Adults." *PsychCentral blog* (blog), *PsychCentral.* November 9, 2022. https://psychcentral.com/blog/the-importance-of-play-for-adults.

Miller, Kori. 2019. "Flow Theory in Psychology: 13 Key Findings & Examples." *Body and Brain* (blog), *Positive Psychology.* March 23, 2019. https://positivepsychology.com/theory-psychology-flow/.

National Institute of Play. 2014. "Scientific Disciplines Researching Play." *Science of Play* (blog), *National Institute of Play.* 2014. https://www.nifplay.org/play-science/scientific-disciplines-researching-play/.

National Organization for Arts in Health. 2022. "Our Story." National Organization for Arts in Health. Accessed December 23, 2022. https://thenoah.net/about/.

Oppland, Mike. 2016. "8 Traits of Flow According to Mihaly Csikszentmihalyi." *Body and Brain* (blog), *Positive Psychology.* December 26, 2016. https://positivepsychology.com/mihaly-csikszentmihalyi-father-of-flow/.

Proyer, René T, and Willibald Ruch. 2011. "The Virtuousness of Adult Playfulness: The Relation of Playfulness with Strengths of Character." *Psychology of Well-Being: Theory, Research and Practice* 1, no. 1 (2011): 4. https://doi.org/10.1186/2211-1522-1-4.

Proyer, René T. 2013. "The Well-Being of Playful Adults: Adult Playfulness, Subjective Well-Being, Physical Well-Being, and the Pursuit of Enjoyable Activities." *European Journal of Humour Research* 1, no. 1 (2013): 84–98. https://doi.org/10.7592/ejhr2013.1.1.proyer.

Robinson, Lawrence, Melinda Smith, Jeanne Segal, and Jennifer Shubin. 2022. "The Benefits of Play for Adults." *Wellbeing and Happiness* (blog), *HelpGuide.* December 5, 2022. https://www.helpguide.org/articles/mental-health/benefits-of-play-for-adults.htm.

Robb, Alice. 2019. "The 'Flow State': Where Creative Work Thrives." *Worklife* (blog), *BBC*. February 5, 2019. https://www.bbc.com/worklife/article/20190204-how-to-find-your-flow-state-to-be-peak-creative.

Samuels, Michael, and Mary Rockwood Lane. 2011. *Creative Healing: How to Heal Yourself by Tapping Your Hidden Creativity.* Oregon: Resource Publishers.

CHAPTER 8
Schwantes, Marcel. 2018. "This Harvard Scientist Says Being a Rebel and Breaking the Rules Makes You a Better Leader (Try Any of These 8 Things)." *Lead* (blog), *Inc.* June 7, 2018. https://www.inc.com/marcel-schwantes/how-can-you-tell-someone-has-true-leadership-skills-surprisingly-science-says-they-are-rebels-who-break-rules.html.

CHAPTER 9
Dictionary.com. 2022. *Discernment.* USA: Dictionary.com, LLC. https://www.dictionary.com/browse/discernment.

Silvia, Paul J. 2008. "Discernment and Creativity: How Well Can People Identify Their Most Creative Ideas?" *Psychology of Aesthetics, Creativity, and the Arts* 2, no. 3 (2008): 139–46. https://doi.org/10.1037/1931-3896.2.3.139.

Wright, Vinita. 2019. "Creativity and the Ignatian Spirit." *Spirituality* (blog), *Ignatian Spirituality.* September 17, 2019. https://www.ignatianspirituality.com/creativity-and-the-ignatian-spirit/.

CHAPTER 10
Bloom, Linda and Charlie Bloom. 2019. "Self-Trust and How to Build It." *Psychology Today,* September 2019. https://www.psychologytoday.com/us/blog/stronger-the-broken-places/201909/self-trust-and-how-build-it.

Cherry, Kendra. 2020. "Unconditional Positive Regard in Psychology." *Psychotherapy* (blog), *Very Well Mind.* May 10, 2020. https://www.verywellmind.com/what-is-unconditional-positive-regard-2796005.

Dweck, Carol. 2014. "Developing a Growth Mindset." Stanford Alumni. October 9, 2014. 9:37. https://www.youtube.com/watch?v=hiiEeMN7vbQ.

ForCreativeGirls. 2018. "Brené Brown On Using Regret As A Tool For Growth." *Opinions and Lessons* (blog), *ForCreativeGirls.* April 27, 2018. https://forcreativegirls.com/brene-brown-regret-growth/.

Goodreads. 2008. "Quotable Quote." *Alan Alda-Quotes* (blog), *Goodreads*. May 27, 2008. https://www.goodreads.com/quotes/46196-be-brave-enough-to-live-creatively-the-creative-is-the?page=2.

Govier, Trudy. 1993. "Self-Trust, Autonomy, and Self-Esteem." *Hypatia* 8, no. 1 (Winter): 99-120. https://doi.org/10.1111/j.1527-2001.1993.tb00630.x.

internetPoem.com. 2022. "Creativity comes from trust. Trust your instincts. And never hope more than you work." internetPoem.com. Accessed December 23, 2022. https://internetpoem.com/rita-mae-brown/quotes/creativity-comes-from-trust-trust-your-instincts-64808/.

Miller, Andy J. 2017. *Creative Pep Talk: Inspiration from 50 Artists*. San Francisco, USA: Chronicle Books.

O' Toole, Garson. 2019. "Self-Trust is the First Secret of Success." Quote Investigator. Accessed December 23, 2022. https://quoteinvestigator.com/2019/05/25/self-trust/.

Pink, Dan. 2022. "Best of 2022: Dan Pink | The Power of Regret." *The Unmistakable Creative Podcast*. Released December 9, 2022. Podcast, 1 hr 10 min. https://podcast.unmistakablecreative.com/best-of-2022-dan-pink-the-power-of-regret/.

Wall, Cynthia Lynn. 2005. *The Courage to Trust: A Guide to Building Deep and Lasting Relationships*. Oakland, USA: New Harbinger Publications.

CHAPTER 11

Baumeister, Roy F., and Mark R. Leary. "The Need to Belong: Desire for Interpersonal Attachments as a Fundamental Human Motivation." *Psychological Bulletin* 117, no. 3 (1995): 497-529. https://doi.org/10.1037/0033-2909.117.3.497.

Campbell, Emily. 2015. "Six Surprising Benefits of Curiosity." *Greater Good Magazine,* September 2015. https://greatergood.berkeley.edu/article/item/six_surprising_benefits_of_curiosity.

Cherry, Kendra. 2022. "What is Self-Determination Theory?" *Theories* (blog), *Very Well Mind*. November 8, 2022. https://www.verywellmind.com/what-is-self-determination-theory-2795387.

Giles, Jenny. 2022. "Jenny Giles—Creative Rebel." Jenny Giles Creative Rebel. Accessed December 23, 2022. https://jennygilescreativerebel.com.

Lavigne, Geneviève L., Robert J. Vallerand, and Laurence Crevier-Braud. 2011. "The Fundamental Need to Belong: On the Distinction Between Growth and Deficit-Reduction Orientations." *Personality and Social Psychology Bulletin* 37, no. 9 (May): 1185-1201. 10.1177/0146167211405995.

Mackenzie, Barth. 2022. "How to be a Creative Rebel." *Blog* (blog), *Mackenzie Barth*. Accessed December 23, 2022. https://www.mackenziebarth.com/blog/creative-rebel.

Nedkova, Violeta. 2017. "What is a creative rebel?" *Creative Rebels* (blog), *Violeta's*. February 20, 2017. https://violetanedkova.com/blog/what-is-a-creative-rebel.

Novick, Linda. 2007. *The Painting Path: Embodying Spiritual Discovery Through Yoga Brush And Color.* Nashville, TN: SkyLight Paths Publishing.

Pink, Daniel. 2017. "Motivation." The Brainwaves Video Anthology. August 30, 2017. 3:17. https://youtube.com/watch?v=wZySfoNQUPo&feature=shares/.

CHAPTER 12

Cameron, Julia. 2016. *The Artist's Way: 30th Anniversary Edition.* NY: TarcherPerigee.

Lancer, Darlene. 2020. "7 Ways to Cultivate Self-Love." *PsychCentral Blog* (blog), *PsychCentral*. January 30, 2020. https://psychcentral.com/blog/7-ways-to-cultivate-self-love#1.

Mostafavi, Hossein, Sadegh Yoosefee, Seyeed Ali Seyyedi, Maryam Rahimi, and Morteza Heidari. 2020. "The Impact of Educational Motivation and Self-acceptance on Creativity among High School Students." *Creativity Research Journal* 32, no. 4 (September): 378-382. https://doi.org/10.1080/10400419.2020.1821561.

CHAPTER 13

Boyle, Brendan. 2020. "10 Activities to Generate Better Ideas." *Blog* (blog), *IDEOU*. 5th January, 2023. https://www.ideou.com/blogs/inspiration/10-activities-to-generate-better-ideas.

Guest User. 2018. "How to Build a Creative Culture Within Your Organization." *The Uncommon League* (blog), *The League of Analysts Inc.* March 13, 2018. https://www.theuncommonleague.com/blog/2018313/how-to-build-a-creative-culture-within-your-organization.

Hickok, Hannah. 2021. "Why Remote Work Has Eroded Trust Among Colleagues." *Remote Control* (blog), *BBC*. March 18, 2021. https://www.bbc.com/worklife/article/20210315-why-remote-work-has-eroded-trust-among-colleagues.

IBM. 2010. "IBM 2010 Global CEO Study: Creativity Selected as Most Crucial Factor for Future Success." *Cision-PR News Wire.* May 18, 2010. https://www.prnewswire.com/news-releases/ibm-2010-global-ceo-study-creativity-selected-as-most-crucial-factor-for-future-success-94028284.html.

Kouzes, James, and Barry Posner. 2008. *The Leadership Challenge, 4th Edition.* San Francisco, CA: Jossey-Bass.

Landry, Lauren. 2017. "The Importance of Creativity in Business." *Business* (blog), *Northeastern University.* November 9, 2017. https://www.northeastern.edu/graduate/blog/creativity-importance-in-business/.

Paris, Audrey. 2021. "Creativity and Innovation: The Next Big Thing." *Dipnote: Science, Technology, and Innovation* (blog), *U.S. Department of State.* April 21, 2021. https://www.state.gov/dipnote-u-s-department-of-state-official-blog/ creativity-and-innovation-the-next-big-thing/.

SmartStorming. 2018. "The Relationship Between Creativity and Innovation." *Consulting* (blog) *SmartStorming.* February 5, 2018. https://www.smartstorming.com/the-relationship-between-creativity- and-innovation/.

The Age of Ideas. 2022. "Mihaly Csikszentmihalyi." The Age of Ideas. Accessed December 23, 2022. https://theageofideas.com/mihaly-csikszentmihalyi/.

United Nations. 2021. "World Creativity and Innovation Day." United Nations. Accessed December 23, 2022. https://www.un.org/en/observances/creativity-and-innovation-day.

Wigert, Ben, and Jennifer Robison. 2018. "Fostering Creativity at Work: Do Your Managers Push or Crush Innovation?" *Workplace* (blog), *Gallup.* December 19, 2018. https://www.gallup.com/workplace/245498/fostering-creativity-work- managers-push-crush-innovation.aspx.

CHAPTER 14

Dijk, Menno, Grant Davidson, and Valeria Mecozzi. 2022. "What is Creative Leadership?" *Creative Leadership* (blog), THNK. Accessed December 23, 2022. https://www.thnk.org/insights/what-is-creative-leadership/.

Doyle, Leslie. 2019. "Common Leadership Styles & Finding Your Own." *Leadership* (blog), *Northeastern University.* March 7, 2019. https://www.northeastern.edu/graduate/blog/leadership-styles/.

Kouzes, James, and Barry Posner. 2008. *The Leadership Challenge, 4th Edition.* San Francisco, CA: Jossey-Bass.

Naiman, Linda. 2022. "3 Ways to Finding a Creative Breakthrough." *Blog* (blog), *Creativity At Work.* Accessed December 23, 2022. https://www.creativityatwork.com/3-keys-to-finding-a-creative-breakthrough/.

Naiman, Linda. 2022. "Jon Kolko on Creative Clarity and Bringing Creative Thinking into Your Company." *Blog* (blog), *Creativity At Work.* Accessed December 23, 2022. https://www.creativityatwork.com/finding-creative-clarity-out-of-chaos/.

CHAPTER 15

Al-karasneh, Samih Mahmoud, Jubran Saleh, and Ali Mohammad. "Islamic perspective of creativity: A model for teachers of social studies as leaders." *Procedia—Social and Behavioral Sciences* 2, no. 2 (2010): 412-426. https://www.sciencedirect.com/science/article/pii/S1877042810000765

Allen, Rabbi Adina. 2023. "Creativity as spiritual practice." *Spirituality* (blog), *My Jewish Learning*. January 5, 2023. https://www.myjewishlearning.com/article/creativity-as-spiritual-practice/.

Cameron, Janet. 2013. "Plato's Argument: Art is an Imitation of an Imitation." *Philosophy* (blog), *Decoded Past*. September 20, 2013. https://decodedpast.com/platos-argument-art-is-an-imitation-of-an-imitation/.

Catholic Creatives. 2023. "Catholic Creatives: A Community of Co-Creators." Catholic Creatives. Accessed January 5, 2023. www.catholiccreatives.com.

Guruge, Ananda. 2010. *Buddhism Today and Aesthetic Creativity*. Morrisville, CA: Lulu.com.

Jacobson, Nolan Pliny. "Creativity in the Buddhist Perspective." *The Eastern Buddhist* 9, no. 2 (1976): 43-63. http://www.jstor.org/stable/44361450.

Jewish Studio Project. 2023. "Jewish Studio Project." Jewish Studio Project. Accessed January 5, 2023. www.jewishstudioproject.org.

Kolstad, Gabe. 2022. "Why creativity matters in the Church." *Digital Minister Strategy* (blog), *The Unstuck Group*. January 5, 2023. https://theunstuckgroup.com/church-creativity-matters/.

Paul, Margaret. 2016. "The Spiritual Power Of Creativity." *The Blog* (blog), *Huffpost*. October 10, 2016. https://www.huffpost.com/entry/the-spiritual-power-of-cr_b_12427572.

Raising Self Awareness. 2018. "Creativity and Spirituality: What Makes a Soul Unique." Raising Self Awareness. Accessed January 5, 2023. www.raisingselfawareness.com/creativity-spirituality/.

Printed in the USA
CPSIA information can be obtained
at www.ICGtesting.com
JSHW011209170823
46694JS00004B/13